THE UNOFFICIAL GUIDE TO SURVIVING LIFE WITH BOYS

Hilarious & Heartwarming Stories About Raising Boys From The Boy Mom Squad

Edited by

TIFFANY O'CONNOR & LYNDEE BROWN

ISBN: 0692950591
ISBN-13: 978-0692950593 (HCCR Books)

This book is dedicated to the sons of each and every writer who contributed a story in this book. Without all of you this book would not have been possible. Your Parents love you very much.

CONTENTS

INTRODUCTION

BRITON UNDERWOOD
PUNK ROCK PAPA

*W*hen my wife, Diana, became pregnant and stepped away from college, people treated it like the end-all of her journey to get her degree. The decision to put her education on hiatus when she became pregnant with our twins wasn't an easy choice to make. Neither was deciding to go back shortly after our third child turned two. In her first semester back after a four-year absence and birthing three sons, Diana made the Dean's List with straight A's.

I think if anything, becoming a mother helped motivate Diana to pursue the dreams she had before our sons were born. To be a boy mom requires a certain level of patience and understanding. There are times when boys seem to be their own sort of messy little creatures. Every child is different, and I can only speak from the experiences of watching my wife raise the three boys in this house, but a strong stomach is necessary as well. An ability to withstand mystery scents, mud tracks through the house, and the occasional puddle in the kitchen will get you far raising boys.

What the parenting books fail to mention is how innately gross little boys can be. There is no chapter on the quirky things boys seem attracted to doing. If I were to write a parenting book on raising boys, I would include a chapter on the odd similarities between a dog and a little boy. Subcategory on why little boys feel the need to pee on every-thing. In fact, I think a whole scientific study needs to be done on the possibility of boys literally being dirt magnets. They have an uncanny ability to simultaneously track dirt everywhere while attracting it to their hands, faces, and clean clothes.

There is a reason the term 'Mama's Boy' is so timeless. It takes an immense amount of love to cook for over an hour and watch your children show mouthfuls of half-chewed food to each other before laugh-spitting it all over the table. But, it's in the moments after bath time, when our three sons curl closely to their mother as she runs her fingers through their hair that I know they will be mama's boys forever. Watching her kiss their heads while she softly tucks them into their beds, all the while smiling at a story about whale sharks, reminds me of the special bond a mother and son can have.

All boys are innately mama's boys. After my mother had passed, I remembered the tender moments cuddled together just after bath time. The sense of love and protection my mom provided me with when she wrapped her arms around me.

As my wife makes her way from the kids' room, I get to see a different side to the relationship. It is in those moments, where she grabs a second of peace after surviving another day raising three boys, I notice she still has the glow she gained when our twins were born.

There is this transformation a woman undergoes when she becomes a mother. A sort of caterpillar to butterfly change, leaving them forever different and somehow more beautiful than you ever imagined they could be. It's an amazing transition where they gain this glow about them. You see them in this new light. No longer just a woman, but a mother.

For the first month of our relationship, the future mother of my children decided we would take things slow. Not wanting to rush into anything, we held off on engaging in sexual intercourse. When the ultrasound technician identified two little heartbeats on the ultrasound, I could see Diana thinking we should have abstained longer. I could be wrong, but I believe I saw her wishing she had left our first date before the appetizers came out.

As her belly grew to proportions I didn't think possible for someone only 4'11", excitement set in. We were going to be parents to twin boys! We debated whether they would need their own cribs, their own clothes, on how to dress them and what sports to encourage them into. The perfect nuclear family played out in our heads as we prepared for their arrival brimming with the optimism and excitement of all first-time parents.

I don't think it was until after our third son was born that my wife fully understood how raising a house of boys would be. I say this because shortly before our third son was born, my wife turned to her OBGYN and wanted a hundred percent confirmation when her tubes were tied she wouldn't have to worry about getting pregnant again. She asked for the confirmation in writing and, shortly before her scheduled C-section began, she reminded her OBGYN to tie her tubes tight.

I realized my wife's capacity to love when the boys became toddlers, and she had to juggle her studies with pretending to enjoy looking at bugs. While dating, I never thought of how good of a mother Diana might be. Although looking back, she always had all the characteristics I would correlate with being a good mother. She is one of those people who is naturally nurturing. Other people's needs come first to her, as she radiates a particular kindness growing rare in the world these days.

While all families are different, the stories in this anthology will highlight the propensity to love that comes with being a boy mom. You will learn you aren't alone; all boy moms have sticky surfaces. One of the things I struggled with when writing this was trying to describe the act of raising boys concisely. I realized I didn't have to.

As one writer in this book describes raising boys,
'It is exhaustingly beautiful and never boring.'

As I hang outfits in the closet that our children will wear to her graduation this summer, Diana looks over different grad school applications she intends to send out. My wife going back to school after so many years doesn't come up nearly enough in conversation. Her making the Dean's List doesn't come up at all. She doesn't mention them, preferring to tell stories of something one of her sons recently did. They seem important to mention here because they highlight the determination and drive of the woman my children are lucky to call their mom. And while she may still make sure at check-ups that her tubes are tied, I like to think if my wife knew she would be a mother to three boys before our first date, she would have sat through the whole dinner.

Buckle Up and Hold On Tight

Amber Christensen

*Originally Published in Memoirs of Mayhem:
The Good, The Bad, and The Hilarious.

*E*ight-year-old Jackson was repeatedly kicking his soccer ball at the front door because it was too cold to play outside, the constant banging of which resonated throughout the house. Blake, the six-year-old, was growling at his four-year-old brother Aaron, who was breathing down his neck trying to watch him play the Nintendo DS.

Aaron wanted me to play catch with him and his new blue mitt for the seventeenth time. But I was too busy discovering a pain worse than stepping on a Lego as eleven-month-old Alex wrapped his tiny fingers around a lock of my long brown hair and used it to pull himself up. *Um, ouch!*

I needed a breather, so I left the chaos to my husband Nick and went for a drive in the dismal December darkness. I drove around and thought about how I used to be so good at life. I graduated from college, lived in Europe, and once held a well-paying job. I also had lofty ambitions for what my children would be like: perfect. It couldn't possibly be that hard to raise quiet, polite, hard-working, respectful, organized, clean, and loving geniuses.

The most entertaining part about my ideals was that before my first little bundle of boy entered the world, I actually believed them. In the beginning, things went well; then we brought him home from the hospital.

Parenthood makes me feel like I know absolutely nothing about anything and rubs that fact in my face daily. I love my kids, but the incessant noise and craziness a house full of boys creates can darn near do me in. I raise my voice too frequently, hide the Candyland cards that send our gingerbread men back to the bottom of the board so the game will end faster, and blissfully ignore my kids when they hit the play button again after their Mickey Mouse movie ends. What's wrong with letting them watch it over and over again as long as they're learning colors and numbers?

My ideals have gone from perfection to, "It's okay if you're wearing two different shoes and only one sock. Just get in the car!"

I once heard a story about a little boy who wakes up on his mom's birthday and decides to make her a chocolate cake. He sets a bowl on the counter then fills a cup full of flour, dusting the floor with white powder as he carries it across the kitchen, and dumps it in the bowl. Next, he adds some cocoa and vegetable oil, a cold cube of butter, and a hefty helping of sugar. The boy climbs onto the counter to mix his concoction and stirs as fast as he can. As he stirs with all his might, flinging batter everywhere, his dad appears. The boy follows his father's eyes around the room, from the flour on the floor to the batter all over the counter to his cocoa-stained face, and realizes in his attempt to make something good he has created a disaster.

Motherhood, despite my good intentions, often leaves me feeling like I'm making a huge mess. Yet, I'm supposed to be the one restoring order. My shortcomings bulldoze my confidence, and I don't always like the person I am at the end of the day. Sometimes I wonder how my husband still loves the mess I see in the mirror. My family deserves someone who patiently gives them her all, not someone who steals the good candy out of their Halloween buckets after they go to bed then shamelessly goes back for seconds.

But, we are good at Friday night pizza parties that end with everyone watching a movie from the inside of a blanket fort. We also take the kids to shoot hoops and go swimming at the city rec center fairly often, so at least we're promoting an active lifestyle. Last but nowhere near least, the three kids I've potty trained are all still alive (even though the first round took an entire year). Three down, one to go!

If there's one absolute truth about parenting, it's that it is full of ups, downs, and a lot of in-betweens. So buckle up, hold on tight, and prepare for a roller coaster ride through the good, the bad, and the hilarious.

So You Are Having a Boy?

Carrie Tinsley

"This morning, my son stepped on one of his own
Legos and sobbed at the unending pain of it all.
All I could think was, Karma." ~Carrie on Y'all

My husband's text message pinged into my phone an hour before the appointment: "Sorry, babe. Stuck in a meeting. Can't take the boys during lunch." If this were any other time, I wouldn't have panicked. I could delay a grocery trip or bring them into a store for a 3-minute emergency diaper run. But this was different.

Today was my yearly gynecological exam. As an added bonus, I was new in town and meeting my doctor for the first time. Thanks to this message, I would be taking my two impossibly rowdy boys, Tate (age 4) and Sawyer (age 2), with me.

The waiting room was chock full of pregnant women, a few nervous-looking husbands, and gals who just needed check-ups. With moderately comfortable chairs and soothing, pastel artwork on the pale green walls, it was the kind of quiet, serene atmosphere patients needed before plopping their feet into stirrups and trying not to make eye contact during the breast exam.

I checked in and received ten pages of new-patient paperwork. Ten pages of intimidating, personal questions about past surgeries (three C-sections), exercise (does running after children count?), smoking (nope), and alcohol consumption (yep). A nurse friend once told me that medical professionals automatically double the amount of alcohol patients admit to drinking on their paperwork. If I'm actually honest on the paperwork, are they going to double that amount and call in child services? Should I just lie like everyone else?

My anxiety over the alcohol question was interrupted by incessant beeping. Tate and Sawyer found complimentary granola bars and a space-age mini-fridge that beeped loudly every... single... time... the... door... opened ....BEEP! When I tried to tear Sawyer away, he screamed, so I allowed the annoying BEEP to continue instead of the death screams he emanated when I tried to stop him.

Tate wolfed down a granola bar even though he had just eaten lunch. He was going for another when I told him that we were only allowed one snack per person, which didn't go over well. While I continued with paperwork, the boys pretended the floor was lava (pronounced "wah-va") and climbed from empty chair to empty chair.

A pregnant woman with a basketball belly sat staring at the boys in horror.

"When are you due?" I asked, hoping to divert her attention from the mass chaos.

"Soon," she said nervously. "I'm 38 weeks. This is our first baby..."

"Not too far away!" I said cheerfully. "Congratula—TATE! Get down from there! — Did you find out the baby's gender?—SAWYER! Put down the magazines! You cannot have another granola bar!"

"It's a boy. We're having a boy," she said, eying my progeny as one climbed onto a coffee table, one was underneath, and they pretended to scare each other and scream very loudly. My paperwork was nearly finished.

"So you're having a boy? That's awesome," I said, giving my boys wide-eyed *come here NOW* hand signals they completely ignored. "Boys are so much fun," I smiled. "Sometimes a handful...obviously, but they're great!"

I'm not going to lie. This poor mother-to-be watched my boys and was wondering if it were too late to request a little girl. I handed my completed paperwork to the receptionist and wrangled the boys closer to me.

"Having boys makes you tough," I confessed. "These two have a big sister who is ridiculously easy. I was only a junior varsity parent until this guy"—I hug Tate to me—"was born. He was next-level on everything."

A nurse called my name, and I wished the young mother the best of luck.

On our way down the hall, the boys tried every doorknob...closets, exam rooms I prayed were empty...nothing was off-limits. This was the stuff nightmares are made of: out of control boys and a gynecological exam...simultaneously.

In my exam room, Tate went straight for a small trash can on the floor. He was nose-and-hand-almost-in-the-can when the nurse snatched it away and put it high on the shelf. She explained that it was full of powerful chemicals and was where they placed the post-exam speculums before cleaning. I said a silent prayer of thanks that my 4-year-old hadn't stuck his hand in a container of chemicals to retrieve a tool used to open a stranger's vagina.

As the adorable, patient nurse and I chatted over medical history, the boys found the stirrups ("What are these for?") and gown ("Can I wear this, Mommy?") and the uber-powerful light ("Where is the on-switch, Mommy?"). The doctor's rolling stool became a race car. They found a 3D model of the female reproductive system and nearly snapped off a fallopian tube. They found a tube of ultrasound jelly and attempted to pry open the lid. If you've never fought over ultrasound jelly with a child while simultaneously lying about your alcohol consumption, you're totally missing out.

My new doctor came in, and she was personable, funny, and not at all worried about the havoc my boys had caused in her otherwise calm office. A mother of three herself and therefore accustomed to chaos, she pointed to the gown ("open in the front!") and promised to be back soon.

The only thing worse than completely disrobing in a cold doctor's office with your children asking awkward questions about your body is if those children figure out that the door doesn't lock and escape the room while you are wearing a waist-length, open-in-the-front cotton garment and nothing else.

Tate and Sawyer slung open the door and fled at the precise moment to provide maximum exposure to my lily-white, scantily-clad body for all spectators at the nurses' station. I had planned to flash my doctor and nurse that day, but not the entire staff.

I had a choice to make: retrieve my boys while dressed in open-in-the-front and a sheet covering me from the waist-down OR take the time to re-dress in my clothes and then find some rope to tie my boys into a chair, interrogation-style. I also considered sneaking out, leaving the boys to fend for themselves and scare pregnant women while I enjoyed a hot coffee somewhere.

I was still deciding when my doctor and nurse knocked politely and asked if I were missing anything. My boys came in, each with suckers in their smiling, sticky mouths, holding the nurse's hands.

We agreed to get our show on the road and get through the exam ASAP, though of course, no one wants a long, drawn-out gynecological exam. The nurse and doctor had a completely captive audience as my boys asked question after question about what they were doing and if their mama was okay.

Boys. Just when you're ready to commit murder, they can be so sweet.

Sawyer felt that he could best comfort me while sitting on my stomach for the pelvic exam. Tate stood behind the doctor, watched every move she made, and solemnly asked if his mommy had to come to the doctor "because her pee-pee tail is missing."

To re-dress, I parked myself in front of the closed (but not locked) door so as not to flash any more unsuspecting nurses. I answered more awkward anatomy questions from Tate as best I could. The doctor assured me that all looked fine and she would see me again in a year.

As we exited the waiting room through a sea of pregnant women, a different mom-to-be caught my eye and asked how old my adorable boys were. "We have a little boy on the way," she gushed. "I can't wait. Boys look like so much fun!" She smiled, maybe seeing a bit of her future as a boy mom.

Tate tugged on my shirt as we were talking and handed me a silk flower he had stolen out of an arrangement in the waiting room. I kissed him on his little forehead and stuffed the flower in my purse as we hustled out of there.

This is My Circus, and These Really Are My Monkeys

Lisa Munn

"If we're ever in the middle of a phone conversation
& I suddenly scream "stop choking him!" don't
worry, that's just life with boys."~Sarcastic Mommy

Hi, I'm Lisa, and I'm the mom of four boys. *crowd gasps* I introduce myself like I'm standing nervously in front of a support group because when you have a brood such as mine, people have a way of making you feel like you have a problem. You're constantly met with, "Oh, you poor thing!" or "You know what causes that, don't you?" No, complete and utter stranger, I don't know what causes that. Please enlighten me and my four children in tow. And then there is my all-time favorite: "Are your kids all from the same Dad?" For the record, they are, not that it's any of your business, stranger in the produce section. Please go back to selecting your bananas and leave me and my traveling circus alone. Yes, we are our own little circus. A freak show to some, it would seem. My circus is my normal, and I wouldn't have it any other way.

My husband and I started our family at a very young age. We knew from the beginning that we wanted more than the average family size. When we learned of my first pregnancy, we couldn't wait to find out the sex of the baby. I was born into a family of girls and the color pink. We were ecstatic at the chance of shaking things up a bit with a boy. At nineteen and a half weeks, we anxiously went in for my ultrasound.

Low and behold, the baby was positioned in such a way that they predicted with almost 100% certainty that all that kicking was, in fact, the work of a boy. We would be entering into a world of unknowns and uncertainties. The shopping for everything blue began.

The next eight years would bring three more boys and a house full of testosterone. We were very grateful that our plan of having kids close in age went according to schedule. However, we realized our family was now complete. My hands were full, and I was beginning to feel like I was always pregnant. It's a sad feeling knowing that you will never have a tiny human kicking your insides again, but it was time to count our blessings and start our journey raising these little boys into fine little men.

I was fortunate to be able to stay home with my kids. My husband worked a lot, so I was pretty much home alone with these little people 24/7. My life was a juggling act. Trying to get kids to school, baseball and soccer practices, while still having an infant that needed to keep a schedule, was very challenging. By the time you have your fourth child, it seems like all you do is live in the car. Don't forget all of the eating that you do in there, as well. We had snacks for every age group, including the adults. My 7-passenger Denali was now a traveling kitchen.

Our house was strewn with Hot Wheels cars and tracks, Legos and every kind of ball imaginable. We had a large playroom which also housed a basketball hoop and t-ball set. I'd love to say that everyone got along swimmingly, but I think we all know that's a lie. Boys are rough. Sometimes, ok MOST times, the things being thrown weren't supposed to be thrown. You learn how to react to it. I can catch almost anything thrown at me, without even looking. That's one of the upsides of being a boy mom. I never thought I could be stirring pasta on the stove and catch a ball that was thrown askew from the family room. This is what you get with a house full of boys. This is my normal.

Let's not forget about one thing that is widely associated with boys: Injuries. Being a stay-at-home mom with four boys can be a little nerve-wracking. Let me first say, I hate the sight of blood. I hate hospitals. I hate seeing others in pain. This is not a good combo when you have birthed four boys. Our first major injury was when my eldest had a field trip in Kindergarten that took place at an ice skating rink. Of course, I went along on the field trip because I couldn't wait to take pictures to scrapbook his first time on the ice. As all of his classmates were trying to keep their balance on the ice by holding onto the side of the rink, my son decided that he was ready to just go for it. Well, he went for it, alright. Face first on the ice, blood everywhere. I will never forget the sound of his chin hitting the ice. We landed ourselves in the emergency room with six stitches to his chin and no pictures to document this field trip from hell. Although this outing did not go as planned, it did have a silver lining. This experience was where I began to realize when I'm put into a situation I'm not comfortable with, I can be strong. I didn't feel faint at the sight of him bleeding. I didn't freak out in the hospital. I did what I had to do for him. He brought out a side of me I didn't know I had.

If I didn't have boys, I wouldn't know the joys of the potty training struggle. Should they sit? Should they stand? It doesn't matter because it's all just a mess. You come to grips that your bathroom now needs to be cleaned three times a day, which I'd rather do than keep changing diapers. Ammonia is a lot cheaper than Pampers, right? And now as they are teens, it still needs to be cleaned three times a day, so that doesn't change, but now THEY can clean it.

If I didn't have boys, I wouldn't know what it's like to have to call the window company to have the family room window replaced because someone decided that a little game of baseball in the backyard should now be played with a rock rather than a baseball. For the record, I don't recommend playing baseball this way. It's pretty expensive.

When you have all boys, people have a way, although probably not intended, of making you feel like you're missing out on something by not having a girl. I can honestly say I've never felt that way. Yes, I'll never know what it's like to throw a princess-themed birthday party. But you know what? Race car themed birthday parties can be pretty kick-ass, too. I'll never be painting finger nails & teaching how to apply makeup. I won't be buying hair bows and making perfect ponytails like my mom did for me. There's no sparkly anything anywhere, and there's no sign of pink. And that's ok.

My boys have manners. My boys have emotions. My boys have a lot of love and respect for me, their family and for others. They may fight sometimes, but when all is said and done, these boys will stick up for each other and have each other's backs. As a mother, I couldn't be more proud. As my late Father used to say, grinning from ear to ear, "What would you do without kids?" I always answered this with a laugh or a "Here's a list of things I could do if I didn't have kids!" In reality, I don't know what I would do without kids. Sometimes it feels like they have taught me more than I have taught them. They have made me a better person. I'm lucky to be their ringmaster.

Confessions of a Boy Mom

Rita Templeton

"You never dream you'd have to yell something like "Get your naked butt off your brother's face!"...
but then you have sons." ~Fighting Off Frumpy

Ladies, are you ...

- Perpetually searching for products to eliminate the smell of urine?
- Unbeatable at choosing the most durable clothing and household items?
- Able to swiftly patch up gag-worthy injuries with the confidence and precision of an E.R. nurse?
- In possession of a mental treasure trove of fart jokes?
- Terrific at tuning out excessive amounts of noise?
- Completely unfazed by things like tackling, jumping, and swinging from death-defying heights?
- Constantly begging someone to put their pants on (and to get their hands out of said pants)?

Then congratulations! If you meet three or more of these conditions ... *you might be a boy mom.*

o anyone who isn't, the condition sounds hideous. Believe me, I know: before I became a boy mom (times four!), the mere description of the daily antics presented by a houseful of dudes would have sent me screaming for the hills ... or at least for the nearest form of birth control. Raising boys can be an epic challenge, especially when you have never been one. Like most little girls, I spent a lot of my childhood fantasizing about my adult life, which always included fancy tea parties and spa days and "girl talk" with a smaller version of myself by my side. The thought of having a son never crossed my mind – not because I didn't *want* a son, but because I had a much better idea of what I'd do with a daughter. I knew what it was like to be a girl, to have a mother-daughter relationship. I had no idea what it was like to be a boy or raise a boy or relate to a boy. So at the big gender-reveal ultrasound during my first pregnancy, you could have knocked me over with a feather when the technician typed "IT'S A BOY" on the screen over a vaguely genital-shaped protrusion.

"My daughter has ... a penis?" I gasped. The technician laughed. I didn't.

At that moment, all the mother-daughter bonding I'd dreamed about crumbled (much like the expensive eye shadow palette my sons would later accidentally destroy). I wasn't disappointed, but I was shocked. I had been so sure of my daughter-filled destiny that I had been openly referring to this baby as "Carly." Carly, who had a frilly pink dress already hanging in "her" nursery closet. Carly, who was not a Carly at all. My self-assured parenting plan was now swirling with doubt; I didn't know the first thing about teaching a boy to be a man. I thought sons were a father's domain. Would I have to be the secondary parent, the one who did the menial tasks like preparing meals and wiping butts and then watching wistfully from the sidelines as my son bonded more with his dad?

But having a son – or a whole bunch of them – proved to be like a whole lot of the uncertainties we fear: scary until it actually happens. You think you can't do something. You're positive you'll be underequipped for the job. And then ... you do it and realize you're not only equipped, you're *good*. You're meant for this. I know now in my bones that I, the girl who spent her childhood dreaming of daughters, was meant to mother males. Who'd have thought? Sure, being a boy mom is an adventure. It's like having a bunch of huge, ravenous, energetic, clumsy, affectionate puppies running around. They will wrestle within the "ring" of your living room like someone's paying them to do it, and they'll knock things over, and leave marks on the wall with various sports equipment (but it won't be too noticeable among the fingerprints and boogers already there). They'll break mirrors and teeth and TV screens and wrists – inadvertently, of course. They'll devour the contents of your refrigerator and pantry until it looks like Mother Hubbard's cupboard, and then ask you what's for dinner. They'll rhapsodize enthusiastically about video games and sports statistics and answer "How was your day?" with a shrug. They'll leave your toilet (and the areas within a two-foot radius) a mess, despite having an *aim-able appendage* to pee with.

If all this sounds hard, that's because it absolutely is; raising sons is not for the faint of heart. Their boisterous exuberance will be overwhelming at times, and to an outsider, it may seem more than a little difficult. In fact, people will literally tell you they feel sorry for you, or marvel that you have your hands full, with the unsaid "Wow, it must suck to have all boys" hanging heavily in the air. Both acquaintances and perfect strangers will nosily inquire if you're going to "try for a girl" and act as though you'll be somehow unfulfilled if you never have one. They react that way because they don't understand how amazing boys actually are (under the smudges of dirt) and how immeasurably our sons change our lives for the better.

Because it's such a tough job, raising boys makes their mothers a unique breed. We become confident and capable in ways we would never have imagined. Boy moms develop constitutions of steel, and we don't bat an eye when we stumble upon creepy-crawlies in pants pockets or crusty, moldy food in bedrooms or must tend to blood-dripping injuries that would make most people feel faint. We become adaptable, gaining an insider's understanding of the male perspective and explaining what things look like from the female side. We get to teach our sons how to be strong *and* how to be tender. We know how big and easily broken their hearts can be, and we get to be their safe, soft place to land when someone breaks them. Best of all, we're the lucky recipients of the boundless love and surprising reverence that boys have for their mamas. There is no loyalty so fierce, no protectiveness so great, than that of a son for his mother – unless maybe it's that of a mother for her son.

I may have expected a daughter, but the universe had other plans. Now when people tell me I "need" a girl (which they do, on an irritatingly consistent basis), I always answer that I wouldn't know what to do with one at this point – and I mean that honestly, having metamorphosed into a boy mom to the core. Not going to lie, there are fleeting moments when I still wonder what having a girl would be like. I think of the sentimental treasures I planned to save "for my daughter." Who will understand the emotional importance of my grandmother's old sewing machine, used to stitch my wedding dress? Who will cherish the American Girl doll I spent countless hours lobbying for my parents to purchase, and even more time playing with? Who will read and re-read the journals wherein I so painstakingly chronicled every juicy detail of my adolescent melodrama?

But then I see a store display of tiny teenage girl shorts that could double as underwear, and I couldn't be more grateful for my burping, farting, jeans-ripping, furniture-destroying, rough-and-tumble brood of dudes.

He's Not a Mama's Boy;
I'm a Boy's Mama

Jorrie Varney

"Being a boy-mom is like being in a tornado.
You worry your insurance won't cover the
damage and half your stuff ends up in the
neighbor's yard." ~Close to Classy

J'm seated at the kitchen table, drinking coffee, when he walks in from outside, sweat on his brow and dirt covering his hand. As he approaches a proud smile grows across his face. He extends his hand and presents me with a single, mangled, half-dead dandelion. While some would consider this nothing more than a common garden weed, to a mother, this gesture is one of the truest symbols of love.

My three-year-old son is *"all boy"* as they say, rough and tumble from head-to-toe. He is dirty, and sticky, and as wild as a pack of raccoons, but under all the grime and male bravado, lives the sweetest soul I have ever known.

I became a mother for the first time five years ago with the birth of my daughter. She is a free-spirit who brings me *constant* joy. We are simpatico, her and I. When I learned I was pregnant with my son, it was hard to imagine my heart could hold any more love. I worried I could never love another child as much as I love my daughter. Our relationship was so precious—her soul a mirror image of my own. How could anything ever come close to what we shared? But then he was here, and it was as if he always had been. There had always been a space in my heart, reserved just for him; I just hadn't known it.

It's been said that there is nothing like the relationship between a mother and her son, and while I might have argued this before he was mine, I can say now, with absolute certainty, this is true.

Since the moment we met, we've shared a special connection. Where my daughter and I are *so* similar, he and I are *so* different, yet somehow we fit together perfectly—he is the peanut butter to my jelly. It takes nothing more than a look, or a touch, for us to understand one another. Of course, I still like to yell about mud on the carpet, or a spilled drink in the kitchen, from time to time, but that's just the *mama* in me.

My boy is good at many things, but sleeping is not one of them. You might say, he's a child of the nocturnal variety. Because of his borderline-neurotic sleep schedule, we became accidental co-sleepers early on. I'm a firm believer in sleeping, so I don't care where you do it, as long as you do it. My bed, your bed, a basket on top of the refrigerator—don't care. As long as you're sleeping, mama is happy.

Now, three years later, he stills sleeps next to me, every night. While this has definitely brought us closer together, it's about as awful as it is amazing. I mean, I love all the snuggles, but I'm not a huge fan of anyone shoving their cold, tiny feet in the back of my underwear at 3 am. Or the restless thrashing that always seems to leave me injured. I love him despite his sleeping behaviors, and I let him torture me every night because sleeping next to me is where he is most comfortable.

My husband says I'm soft, not the squishy-extra-skin sort of soft, (although that would also be an accurate description) but the *"you let the kids get away with murder"* soft. If it were up to him the little man would be out on the streets. OK, not the actual streets, but he would definitely be forced to sleep in his own bed. Not me though, I'm wrapped tightly around the proverbial finger. If he feels most comfortable sleeping next to me, then so be it. He won't want to sleep next to his mama when he's a teenager; I'll probably lose my cool-mom status long before then, so you won't see me turning him away at the gate.

The truth is, I rarely tell him no unless he is going to die or kill someone else, which happens more than you might think. I don't give him everything he wants, but most people would probably say he's spoiled. Most people would call him a mama's boy. He's only three, so it's not too hard to spoil him, it really only takes an extra pack of fruit snacks and some chocolate milk, and I'm the greatest mom ever. I'm his favorite, and I like it that way.

When he crashes his bike, it's me he calls out to. I dry his tears, give him a Band-Aid and a pep-talk, and send him on his way, good as new. "Thanks, I love you, mommy." He says as he runs back outside. Aside from half-dead dandelions, "I love you, mommy" is where it's at. If I heard it 100 times a day, it would never be too much. Little boys are great for your self-esteem.

I've been living the good life for three years now, but the tide has started to turn as my son grows from toddler to little boy. He has discovered that daddy also loves dirt, loud machinery, and fart jokes. He has started to stray from my side, in favor of a rowdier crowd—the daddy crowd. As a mother, I am both overjoyed and terribly sad to watch the sweet relationship between my husband and my son blossom. It is everything you would want a father-son relationship to be, and if he grows up to be just like his daddy, the world will gain another beautiful, kind man. It's silly to be sad, but I know this means he won't need me as much as he once did. He won't need me to kiss his boo-boos, or dry his tears. He won't need me to hold him during spring thunderstorms, or when he's had a bad dream. He's becoming exactly who I hoped he would be—a strong, happy, independent boy...but I'm just not ready.

Some may call him a mama's boy, but the truth is, he just a boy, and I'm his mama. I would walk through fire for any of my children if it meant they were safe and happy. I will always feel this way, no matter how old they are, or how little they really "need" me. When my son comes home from college with an empty belly and a basket full of dirty laundry, I will gladly wash his dirty socks, make his favorite meal, and send him back with a giant plate of cookies, because that's what a mother does—she takes care of her babies. He will always have a piece of my heart, and I will always be there for him because I'm that boy's mama.

PEOPLE OF WALMART

TIFFANY O'CONNOR

"My friend asked me what it was like to live in a house full of boys, so I peed on her bathroom floor, ate everything in her fridge, told her 800 stories about Minecraft, farted 20 times and when she was ready to kill me I gave her a hug and told her she was pretty." ~#Lifewithboys

I was six months pregnant with my first child the day I jinxed myself. I was wandering around the baby department at Walmart comparing diapers. I was trying to decide if my baby would be more comfortable pooping in the diapers that claimed to be blanket soft or if he would prefer the ones made with breathable mesh when I ran into the brattiest toddler I had ever seen in my life. He was lying on the ground screaming for candy. His very pregnant, desperate mother spoke to him in a frantic whisper, begging him to get off the floor and to quit making a scene. She reached down several times to try to pick him up, but each time she got close he would snarl and kick in her direction.

Eventually, she caved in and handed him a candy bar. She looked exhausted and defeated. He consented to be placed in the cart and joyfully devoured his treat. He seemed very pleased by the fact that he had broken his mother's will. I rubbed my belly and told my little man that we would never behave that way. I would be a good mother, and he would be a well-behaved child. I believe that he must have heard me because he never had a tantrum in the store. Instead, he found ways to make me wish that I was the mother of the naughty screaming toddler because that would somehow seem more normal than my son's future Walmart behavior.

The first incident happened shortly after his first birthday. We were standing in the checkout line. I was mindlessly flipping through a magazine, and he was sitting in the cart being a perfect angel, or so I thought until I felt a bony finger tap me on the shoulder. I looked up from my magazine and found my son holding a package of raw hamburger meat and gobbling it down like a little Mogwai eating after midnight right before becoming a Gremlin. There were several old ladies behind me who were giving me very dirty looks. I picked him out of the cart and rushed him to the bathroom to rinse out his mouth.

I was positive he was going to die of mad cow disease. I felt like the worst mother in the world. It got even more embarrassing when the adorable teenage cashier, upon finding the package open, apologized and offered to get me a new package of hamburger and I had to explain to her that I had to buy that package because my child had just eaten half of it.

When he was two, we started potty training. I bought him one of those cool potty seats. It was soft and white, and he absolutely loved it. It became his favorite hat. I'm not joking, he refused to sit on it, but he insisted on wearing it everywhere we went for about three months. I don't care how many crazy people of Walmart things you have seen. You haven't seen it all until you see the exhausted mother of a toddler walking around the store with her child in his potty hat. People would stare at us as if we were exhibits in a freak show.

Eventually, he did succumb and learned to use the potty. This lead to our next incident. I was shopping for a Valentine's Day card for my husband. I looked down to ask my three-year-old who was holding my hand which card he wanted to give daddy. What I observed was him with his pants around his ankles peeing all over the display of birthday cards. I was too ashamed to even tell an employee what he had done. We left immediately, and to this day I still have never been back to that specific Walmart. I imagine they have my picture hanging on the wall like a wanted poster with some description about how I let my kid pee on the merchandise.

As my son grew older, he found more and more ways to make me wish I hadn't judged that other mother. There was the time when he was four, and I was pregnant with his brother when we walked past a very nice family and after playing peek-a-boo with their baby he loudly announced that he wanted his brother to be a brown baby and not a peach baby. He told me brown babies were prettier than peach babies. I told him that we couldn't pick out his brother's skin color and that the baby in my belly would be peach like him. He then informed me that I could buy him a brown baby and he continued throughout the store screaming at me super loudly to buy him a brown baby. We got several horrified looks.

There was another time when he was convinced that an older lady we walked past was a troll and got excited and pointed at her screaming "Mama, mama it's a troll." Let me tell you; she was not amused. The look she gave me was probably the same look that a troll would give Billy goats right before it ate one of them.

Then there was the time he refused to leave the store for ten minutes because it was raining and someone at school had told him that rain was God peeing and he did not want to get peed on. He also yelled at everyone who walked past him out into the rain and let them know that they were getting peed on. I couldn't decide if I was mortified or amused.

The most recent incident occurred a couple of years ago. I had gone to a Fifty Shades of Grey charity event with some friends. After a few glasses (ok a few bottles) of wine, we decided to create our own list of hard limits. Mine was a very uncomfortable place that isn't the back of a Volkswagen (if you get the Mallrats reference). I used a crayon and a cocktail napkin to write down our list and then absentmindedly threw it in my purse. So later, while looking for gum in my purse my son found the napkin, I had forgotten it even existed. He asked me loudly why we couldn't have a lizard. When I looked at him confused, he waved the napkin around in front of everybody in Walmart and said, "See you wrote no anole like the lizard, why don't you like Lizards Mom?" This is the only time in my life I have been happy that he wasn't a great reader. However, the sixty-something-year-old cashier had no problems reading it.

The moral of all of this (other than that my son and I should be banned from Walmart for life) is that we need to stop judging each other as mothers. We are all just doing the best we can every day. We all have our own bad mommy moments. When we question if we are even cut out for motherhood, but if you love your kids fiercely you are. My oldest is 13 now. He is compassionate, hardworking, and well behaved according to his teachers. He survived all of our incidents at Walmart and still turned out ok. So now when I see a mother trying to deal with her own Walmart incident, I give her a smile and let her know it's all going to be ok.

THEY MAKE GREAT PETS

SUZANNE FLEET
(With special credit to Hadley Fleet)

*"With soap is not something I should
have to say after wash your hands. That's
life with boys" ~Toulouse & Tonic*

*I*magine a home -- yellow with a big white front porch, a deck on the back - and a giant yard to run in. Inside the house, it's comfy and cozy, and there's already a special place prepared for the new family member. Then picture a mom, with yellow hair just like me and arms spread open - and a dad who likes to get down on the floor and tussle.

My name is Hadley, and I'm that lucky girl.

I'm the daughter of a wonderful mom named Suzanne who takes exceptional care of me, feeds and snuggles with me, and even works at home so she can be there for me.

My dad's name is Gabe, and he works a lot because *this house is not going to pay for itself.*

When mom and dad brought me home for the first time, they showed me all over my new house, including my own special bed. I settled in quickly, doing what little ones always do. I peed and pooped everywhere -- and loved listening to the sound of my mommy's tinkling laugh as my dad wretched while cleaning up his share of the messes. Daddy has a hair-trigger vomit reflex. It's a family trait. I gag on something pretty much every day.

As I said, there was little more I could ask for. It was the perfect home, the perfect family. Except for one thing.

When I came home that first time in my mother's arms, I discovered that mom and dad had a loud, squawking, spoiled pet called a "boy."

His name is Asher, and he'd already been there for three years when I joined the family. And not in the yard where he clearly belonged either but inside, with free roam of the house.

It took some time to get used to the habits of this exotic pet, but I worked to adapt for the sake of the family. Then just when we were all falling into a rhythm, my parents came home from a trip with another boy. And this time, it was a newborn!

The chaos was inconceivable. Meyer screamed bloody murder at all hours. Almost as soon as I'd fall asleep at night or for a nap, I'd find myself lifting my head up in alarm and turning my ears from side to side, tortured by the high-pitched sound of his cries.

It's hard to describe the mess this made of my perfect family for close to 14 years. But at last, the new boy grew and was able to move around without being carried -- although even then he fell constantly as though he were sucking Mommy Juice out of his drinking bottle all day.

Finally, the sounds Meyer emitted began to resemble those of our other boy, Asher - so while still annoying, they were at least in a lower pitch. Life with our pets became more bearable, occasionally even enjoyable.

If you're considering adding a boy to your family, let me offer you the benefit of my experience.

First of all, boys are not quiet nor inexpensive pets. They're either eating or making noise constantly. And even though my parents got them to keep each other company, they fight and bicker far more than they get along. When we had one boy, it wasn't uncommon for him to whine, but now that we have two, we often have to physically pull them apart. There are scratches, bumps, bruises, and cuts on a regular basis. I know what you're thinking: obedience school. Well, it's doing zero for these two if you ask me.

Secondly, boys are loving pets but don't know their own strength. They're rough with the touch, completely lacking in gentleness, and often pull on my arms, legs, and ears. Occasionally they even have the nerve to tug on my rear end! But I get them back for that one, trust me.

You should also keep in mind that these are naturally competitive creatures who will clash over even the most ridiculous things. In fact, our boys have an ongoing argument about whether my favorite color is blue or orange. "No, it isn't." "Yes, it is!" "Nu-uh!" "Uh-huh!" I mean, just ask me. I like yellow.

Finally, boys are high-maintenance pets, especially when it comes to my mother's attention. They love her a little too much for my taste, and it seems like I'm always waiting for my turn to sit in her lap or get fed or be snuggled. It's just stupid that I have to wait until the pets go to bed to turn a few circles and cuddle up next to her on the couch.

Now that I've given you the downsides to having this species called boys as pets, here are some upsides I've discovered with some deep, deep digging.

Boys love to eat - they're shoving food in their faces as long as they aren't asleep. Plus ours seem to think the floor is the garbage can. Put two and two together, and there are often lots of extra goodies to be had if you keep your nose to the ground.

You'll find that this choice of pet is also messy in all the right ways. They play fast and loose with all bodily emissions. More than once, my mom has called one of their names while he was urinating into the pet potty, only to have him turn his whole body towards her, peeing on the rug. And you'll never find another pet so devoted to farting, pooping and talking about farting and pooping. One time, I accidentally passed gas so loudly, I scared myself and ran away. My boys laughed so hard that one of them farted too! Never a dull moment.

Boys likewise have a delightful, persistent odor all their own. It's easy to find piles of clothes that reek of them on the floor in any room. This makes for an exceptional place to nap when they're away.

Lastly, when I'm feeling frisky, my boys are always ready to play tug-of-war or a game of hide and seek. They can also learn simple tricks like sitting or fetching but usually forget them almost immediately.

In the end, despite their eccentricities, boys make great pets. There are more sophisticated options, of course, but if what you're looking for is a boisterous, loyal pet for your children to play with, boys are the way to go.

"Mom, I Have to Go Pee!"

Jennifer Martin

*"A boy is truth with dirt on its face, beauty with
a cut on its finger, and the hope of the future
with a frog in its pocket." ~Mom Vs. The Boys*

With my youngest son due for an appointment with the optometrist, I found myself enjoying a morning in the city with just my little guy. He did an amazing job getting his eyes checked out, was a fun little shopping buddy while we ran some errands and I had decided to treat him to a lunch date before we headed home. In big families, any chance to steal some one-on-one time is special, and I wasn't in a hurry for our time to end.

Heading into the restaurant, we chose a booth by the window so my son could watch the big trucks go by and I could keep an eye on the weather, a snow storm was brewing, and we still had to make the drive back home.

"Mom, I have to go pee!"

Boy moms know how frustrating it can be when you are out on the town, and one of the boys' shouts out those dreaded words. When my boys were little, I would just drag all three of them into the ladies room with me, but it didn't take too long before they started to complain and demanded to use the men's room instead.

Look, I get it, no male wants to hang out in a ladies washroom, and they've received some pretty rude looks in the past from little girls who were in there and didn't understand why these boys just came into their space. But as a parent, it can be a tough step to let them wander off solo into a space you aren't allowed to tread yourself.

Having more than one boy definitely helps and because I have three when one of the boys asks to use the washroom in a restaurant or store, I always just send one of the other brothers with them. Safety in numbers right ladies?

But on this particular day, the buddy system wasn't going to work, and it gave me pause. My husband and I are big on giving the boys opportunities to test their independence, so I assessed the situation and decided he was fine to go on his own. Due to the cold day and the amount of snow coming down outside the window we appeared to be the only ones in the restaurant, but even still without a direct line of sight to the restroom door, I decided to trail along after him. I stayed back at the end of the hallway and watched as he found the right door and ducked in. I watched a nearby T.V. broadcasting information on the local road conditions, time ticked on.

What was taking so long? It felt like forever since he had gone in there. I decided to walk down the hallway and stood just outside the door to the men's room. Now I could hear his voice coming from the other side of the door. Who was he talking too? My mind started to race. Was there someone already in there when he went in? His voice was getting louder, was he yelling? What the heck is going on in there?

And just as I was about to bust through that men's room door, he opened it.

His little face looked up at me, quite surprised to see me standing in the doorway and giggled.

"What are you doing mom?" he asked

"I was just checking on you" I replied

"Oh, did you hear me?" he wondered

"I did hear you, who were you talking to?" I questioned

"No one, I was dancing in the mirror, like this, watch" and he started to boogie down as I started to hear the music coming from the bathroom speakers that was now flooding into in the hallway.

A mom's anxious mind can turn a million scenarios a second when something doesn't seem quite right with our kids, but boys often just don't have a care in the world While I was pacing outside the washroom door, he was in there throwing himself a dance party, with loud singing to boot! That little wild child of mine certainly keeps me on my toes.

Signs of a Concussion

ASHFORD EVANS

*"Every morning at 6:30 AM my little man
sneaks into my room, crawls into my bed, snuggles
down, takes my face in both of his hands, and
when we are nose to nose he whispers to me,
"Mommy you have bad breath," This is how I
start every single day!" ~Biscuits and Crazy*

The first rule of having boys is to develop a thick skin. They are rough, they are wild, and they smell funny. You have to learn to let things roll off your back. To not jump at every precarious move. To ignore the smell of pee. You should also probably consider getting your EMT certification or at the very least take a first aid course. It could end up saving you in the end.

Case in point:

The other night the kids and I are all sitting around the dinner table. I must have blinked or something because all of the sudden Meeny (my three-year-old) managed to take a flying leap from his booster seat and catapult himself directly onto his forehead on the hard wood floor. The poor thing didn't even have time to put his hands out to break the fall. Immediately a dinosaur-sized goose egg popped up on his head. Of

31

course, being the hypochondriac that I am, I immediately thought he for sure had a concussion. The hubs is working late every night this week, and so I am flying solo with all three kids. I began to panic.

Naturally, I did what I always do in a crisis and called the closest medical professional that I know. My dad. Who, in fact, is a dentist.

"DAD! Meeny just busted his head on the hardwood floor! How do I know if he has a concussion?" I screamed desperately into the phone.

"Um. I don't know is he acting weird?" my father flatly replied.

"HE'S three!!! YES, he's acting weird. Everything he does is weird!" I said.

"Sweetie, why don't you just Google it?"

"Aren't you a medical professional? Why are you telling me to Google it?!"

"Are his teeth ok?"

"What? Yes, his teeth are fine it's his head I'm worried about!"

"Well, I'm a dentist, so if his teeth are ok I think you should Google 'Signs of a Concussion'"

"Thanks, Dad glad we had this talk," I said with disgust as I slammed down the phone and grabbed my laptop. I typed in "Signs of a Concussion" into the search bar and found a laundry list of symptoms.

Let's break this down in terms of a three-year-old's behavior:

1 Brief loss of consciousness- Nope didn't experience that as evidenced by the ear-piercing banshee like screams only muffled by the dense hardwood smashed against his lips

2 Memory loss- This one is a little tricky. How does one measure "Memory Loss" in a three-year-old? I mean we call the kid "Sundowners" because every time he wakes up, he demands breakfast. Now, this would be normal in the mornings, but he also does it after naps.

Sometimes I give in and make him eggs for an afternoon snack because I just don't have the energy to battle it anymore.

3 Confusion- Again a slippery slope. As I was putting him to bed tonight, he started crying because he wanted to make his "Lego helicofter." I told him it was time for bed and that we could work on it tomorrow. "NOOOOOOOO," he screamed. "I DON'T WANT TO DO IT TOMORROW I WANT TO DO IT IN THE MORNING!!!!!" Um....okay. Well, I'm confused at least.

4 Drowsiness or feeling sluggish- This has NEVER been the case with Meeny. He's the type of kid that gets amped up when he gets over tired. It's awesome. Picture running full speed straight into the wall, crashing into it, bouncing back so hard his feet flip over his head in a back roll. He stands up shakes his head and does it again towards the other wall. THIS is the way MY child exhibits exhaustion.

5 Dizziness- See above.

6 Nausea or vomiting- Nope not tonight although he does vomit if you look at him cross-eyed on most days. This kid has the weakest stomach of anyone I've ever seen (besides my husband).

I once reached ninja-level parenting when we were in the middle of a crowded Five Guys, and I saw the early stages of a puketastrophe. I quickly grabbed the fry cup, dumped the fries out on the table, and held the cup over his mouth just as he let loose. No one in the restaurant was any the wiser. We discreetly discarded the defiled cup and went about the rest of our meal.

7 Sensitivity to light/noise- So I can't even flush the toilet until he leaves the room because "IT HURTS MY EARRRRRSSSSSS!!!!" How would one measure an increased sensitivity in a case such as this?

8 Balance problems- Really? Under normal circumstances, he can't walk more than five steps without tripping over his own feet and plummeting to the ground.

9 Slowed reaction to stimuli- Well that depends. Is the stimuli the sound of my voice? Particularly when I'm giving some sort of over complicated instruction such as "Hold your pee-pee down while you're on the toilet." This versus the sound of my voice saying "You may have one piece of candy." It's all relative I guess.

I believe that there should be some sort of adjusted toddler concussion scale on WebMD. Or at least an adjusted boy mom scale. Because this list was simply useless. So I kept him up a little later than usual (regretting every minute of it) and finally put him to bed. He seemed fine the next morning- I guess we'll figure out in a few years if any real damage occurred.

MUD, BLOOD, AND *HARRY POTTER*

KAREN JOHNSON

"Take your hands out of your pants &
don't lick your brother. –Things I say
in church"~21ˢᵗ Century SAHM

*W*hen you don't grow up with brothers, the concept of "boys," especially "little boys" is a mysterious one. Sure, I had childhood friends who were boys, and I dated a teenage boy or two in high school, but the only "boys" I have ever lived with are my dad and my husband—both of whom are grown-up boys.

So one day in June of 2008, when the ultrasound technician pointed to a penis on the screen next to me, I thought to myself, "Okay…" and wondered what the hell I was in for.

Having only one sister, I was raised in a very tidy and organized house exclusive to Barbies, dance costumes, and glitter. My Saturdays were spent lip-syncing to Madonna and Paula Abdul, painting my nails, and doodling in my diary. My parents signed me up for sports, but my true skills were keeping the bench warm and doing cartwheels in the outfield. I've never broken a bone or even had stitches. After all, playing house and school isn't very far into the danger zone.

And now, at 28 years old, I was going to live with a little boy for the first time. *What if he loved mud and dirt and spiders and guns? Boys pee outside and like video games and jumping off stuff. And their feet always, always smell.*

I thought.

And I was right.

But not at first.

Because I did have a boy in November of 2008 and he *is* now a video-game lover (something I've had to accept, with my husband's encouragement that "he'll be fine"). But as a toddler, he wasn't the "boy" I'd anticipated. While the other boys at play dates cannon-balled off of the couch, mine was in the corner reading. While they tore through the aisles at the grocery store, knocking over pickle jars, mine read all the nutrition labels to me and counted the squares on the floor.

I'll admit that I unfairly judged the mothers of those crazy boys. At the park, I would watch in horror as they aggressively climbed backward up the slide and pushed other kids down. It had to be their parenting, I thought. They clearly have no control. Then (from atop my pedestal of parenting smugness) I'd look over at my son and smile proudly as he carefully slid down the slide (the right way) while reciting his ABCs.

I maintained my comfortable position on top of sanctimommy-mountain for four blissful years. In 2010, we welcomed our peaceful little girl into the world. An all-night sleeper from day one and a baby who hardly cried, she meshed nicely into our quiet, organized family of four. My son, who was now two, practiced his letters and numbers daily. He flipped through book after book after book while other boys drew on couches with Sharpies and threw plastic dinosaurs in the toilet.

So confident were my husband and I in our parenting, that we thought, "Hey, let's give this one more go-round!"

So we did. And four years ago in 2013, our third child entered this world. A boy.

Oh, how karma hurts.

As a 19-lb 4-month old, this child has been what you might call "a challenge" from the very beginning. The wooden blocks neatly stacked by my first son have only ever been chucked across the room by my second. While number one loved learning letters and numbers as a toddler, my youngest would merely grunt. Now a preschooler, he may comply with my wishes to practice writing his name only if I promise an epic light-saber battle immediately after. "Good job writing your D!" I'll say, as I am whacked in the neck with a sword.

At three years old he spent the entire summer with a black eye. Now that he's in preschool, he's visited the nurse weekly. Ice. Band-Aids. More ice. More Band-Aids. She doesn't even bother to call me anymore, and I'm grateful.

In a 24-hour period, he'll melt your heart with love, hugs, and kisses—and flash you dimples to die for. But he'll also hit you in the face with a stick, sneak three candy bars, and rip a hole in his shirt. Even at four, if he's alone and quiet, you had better see what he's up to. I've caught him standing on a step stool *on top of my bed* in the attempt to reach my ceiling fan. He's been known to create towers of stools, chairs, and boxes in the precarious attempt to reach the candy jar atop the refrigerator. There is no mountain he is afraid to climb.

Speaking of treats, on several occasions, we've found him hiding behind the couch, elbow deep in a box of cupcakes or stuffing his face with stolen cookies. One such offense occurred when I was awoken by the sounds of ripping plastic at 3 A.M.

My first son's primary goal in life is to avoid trouble at all costs. To his younger brother, rule-breaking is a life source. He has a temper that could wake a sleeping dragon from a century-long slumber. The most recent casualty is the broken spindle to our upstairs railing. Where there used to be a neat, symmetrical row of white poles, there is now a gaping hole after a certain little boy yanked one out, snapped it in half, and brought it to me, saying "Sorry, Mommy."

Other "Sorry, Mommies" have happened too—like throwing a toy gun mid-tantrum, which means a chunk of wall is now missing or breaking the outdoor storage bin on our patio because he "had to jump off it as a pirate!"

Having a wild boy doesn't mean we "can't have nice things." It means we can't have *things*. Like walls, railings, or storage containers. Remember judgmental me who scoffed at the kid pushing others off the slide and shook my head at the pickle-smasher in aisle three? Yeah… karma.

Nine years into this parenting gig, I feel like a new mom every day, always surprised and slightly terrified of what's coming next. When my second son is in someone else's care, whether it be a friend, family member, or his teacher, I dread the phone call telling me that his 100th jump off the top step was the one that did him in and his teeth are no longer in his face...Or that he "wrestled" another kid a little too hard... Or that I should head on over to the ER with my insurance card.

I am a boy mom, but I am raising two very different boys. So what does #lifewithboys mean in my house?

Mud.

Blood.

ER visits and black eyes.

"He threw a rock at me!" but also, "Let's play a math game on the computer!"

Holes in the knees of brand-new pants.

Dirty cleats and stinky jock-straps.

Marathon games of Monopoly, chess, and Sudoku.

Reading *Harry Potter* five times.

Yelling "No throwing baseballs in the house!"

Science camp by day and soccer practice by night.

Messy hair and dirty fingernails.

Overdue library books.

Tears.

Fears.

And love.

We may have holes in the walls and holes in our pants, but I wouldn't trade this life. It's exhaustingly beautiful and never boring. Someday, my youngest child may have a boy just like him, and when he throws a baseball through the living room window, I'll tell my son that it's okay. He's just a little boy.

Boys Are The Best!

Leslie Means

"I told my son he could be anything he
wanted. He took his pants off and said,
"I want to be naked mommy." Dream big
little one." ~Her View from Home

J saw her coming towards me but couldn't remember her
name. I would blame my brain fog on the 9-week-old, but
truthfully, I'm just terrible at names.

"Leslie! Congratulations on your baby boy!" she exclaimed. "Aren't
boys the best? We're expecting again. Boy number three. I love being
a boy mom!"

It was a lot to take in, especially in my state of delirium. My 9-week-
old was sleeping peacefully in his stroller, and I was trying to shop for
a pair of pants to fit my wider, just had my third baby - hips.

Her comment left me searching for words.

"Thanks," I mustered. "I'm trying to find a pair of jeans before he
wakes up," I added, hoping she would take my hint to let me move
along.

"Well, enjoy that sweet boy," she smiled as she walked toward the
discount rack of shirts.

I grabbed the pants and headed to the nearest dressing room. As
I shimmied myself into this season's latest styles, I questioned her
comment.

Do I love being a boy mom? How was I supposed to answer that comment? Truthfully, I keep forgetting I have a boy. Other than the reminder each time I change his diaper, baby boys are just like baby girls.

They eat. They poop. They cuddle, snuggle, and make hearts ooze with love.

He's been attached to me for the last nine weeks. Certainly, by now I should be used to this boy mom thing.

I'm getting there.

When my husband and I decided to start our family, I knew there would be a girl or two in it. I have three older sisters; I'm the baby girl in a big family. I expected to have all girls too.

When our second daughter was born, my husband and I wondered if our family was complete. Two healthy girls. It seemed like an American dream. And then the comments came in.

"You guys should really try for a boy." "Boys are the best!" "Oh, sad. Are you sure you're done? You would miss out not having a boy!"

Their comments were frustrating.

Six years after our youngest was born, we were expecting again, and the opinions came back.

"Oh! I hope you have a boy," they would say.

I left one mom speechless when I sternly told her that I, "loved being a girl mom and fully expected to have another girl and was very happy about that."

"OK!" she said.

OK.

"Do you see that?" our doctor said during the 20-week ultrasound. "That would make your baby a boy!"

"Wait. What did she say?" my husband asked with excitement.

"A boy," I told him with happy tears in my eyes.

A boy.

"Aren't you excited?" friends asked.

"Yes, but we would have been thrilled either way. We are just happy he's healthy and growing well and that all looks good."

Because that's what a good mom says, right? We just want a healthy baby. Boy or girl, it doesn't matter.

But in my heart, I was secretly thrilled.

Here's my truth. I've been afraid to tell everyone how excited I am to have a boy. As if saying that fact out loud would somehow diminish my love for my girls.

But that's just a lie. A piece of mom guilt my brain is trying to squash. A mother's love isn't biased. It only grows with each baby. You know this because you're a mother. I know this too.

Here's what I should have told the kind boy mom in the store last week.

"Do I love being a boy mom?"

Every snuggle and cuddle and late night diaper change, all the sleepless nights and days, each smile and coo and hazy nursing session, all of it is because of my son.

I love that I see my husband in his eyes. I love his legs rolls and gummy grin. I love every ounce of his little body. And even though I have called him my sweet girl on more than one occasion (hazards of being a seasoned girl mom) I'm starting to get used to this boy mom gig.

And I love it more than I ever imagined.

On the day he was placed in my arms, I was complete. A mother of three. A girl mom and a boy mom. A title I didn't expect to have but am so honored to hold.

Why I Stopped Raising My Sons

Lauri Walker

*"My son just left the house with a smile
and a crow bar. I should probably check
on that" ~Mama Needs a Nap*

When I started having children, I wanted to have girls. All girls. I knew in my heart I was a girl mom through and through. I was going to outfit my future daughters in sweet dresses with shiny shoes and pretty hair bows, and they would grow up to be smart, independent, and beautiful women.

Never mind that *I* was a tomboy through and through and knew absolutely nothing about "girly" stuff.

I had no sense of style, no clue about fashion or hair or makeup. I wore jeans and baggy sweatshirts, and I liked myself that way, but I wanted girls, and I was lucky enough to have one. She was a gorgeous tomboy. After her, the boys tumbled into our lives: one after another, after another, after another.

I became a boy mom. Ready or not.

As each of my sons was born, I had a purpose. I would raise them to be smart, strong, respectful boys. I believed it was up to me to teach them how to think for themselves. I would guide them to treat girls with respect and encourage them to choose their friends wisely, and they would have a quiet confidence that only a mother's love could instill. They would be gentlemen. I would make sure of it.

My boys would be hard workers and would play equally hard. They would focus on their schoolwork and get the best grades that their best effort would earn. They would try every sport and never quit anything. My young men could decide what they enjoyed, and they didn't have to do something they didn't like more than once, but once they started something they had to finish it.

They would be examples in our community. Every other mom would want her child to be friends with my sons. That is how ultimately GOOD I was going to raise my boys to be. It was a good goal and one I still have, but it has shifted some. I am no longer focused on raising my boys. I've looked at them, at what I believe their future holds and decided that my original idea of raising my boys is short sighted. My boys are only going to be my boys for a very short time. It is a tiny, fleeting moment of their lives that I live in the center of and I intend to soak up every second of it. I won't take any of it for granted, and I will do my very best to savor the joy and sweetness of their childhood, even as they run like hell straight on through, but I'm not raising my boys anymore.

I'm raising someone's husband.

I'm raising the fathers of my grandchildren.

My daughter has grown and is on her way out into the world; I know how quickly these moments move away from us. I have what feels like less than a finger snap of time to teach each of my sons what really matters in life. To teach them how to make his wife feel safe when her world feels upside down, how to make her feel like she is the only person in the entire world because she is the most important person in his world, to understand that it is his privilege and honor to partner with her in life rather than rule over her. I want each of my sons to understand how to love and cherish his wife above all others and second only to God.

I will have the blink of an eye to teach these young men how to be a father to their children. How to love and discipline with patience and kindness. How to both succeed and fail as a parent because fail they will. I have to prepare them to know when and how to say "I'm sorry" to their children when they screw up, this parenting gig because they will make mistakes.

My goal as a mom is different now than it was when my children were born. My sons have not been the perfect image of gentlemanly excellence that I had once imagined. They spend too much time on video games, they get into fights with each other on a regular basis, and one of them spends a great deal of time trying to jump his bike off of things like the steps of the police department and roof of the middle school. They get into trouble, they get scraped and bruised, and they get dirty. All of their rooms smell… weird…bad… I try not to go in there.

They also do all of the other things I had hoped and prayed for. All of the GOOD things.

Essentially, they are normal.

As I watch them grow into the men I know they are yearning to become, as I see the set in their shoulders mature, it is easy to imagine their babies riding up there one day. I can picture them standing side by side with a wife, a partner in life, and knowing how to honor her.

They are still boys, and they still need the guidance from their father and me, even as they fight against it, but every day I see the men they will be shining in their eyes, and I am happy to have changed my course as a mom. Raising boys isn't what I thought it would be. We've had our share of dead animals, bugs, dirt, and dump trucks, but I wasn't quite prepared for the weight of the responsibility of preparing them to be the provider, the head of the household, the life partner, and each a man of God.

I'm in now. Ready or not.

DIFFERENT IS INTERESTING

AMANDA RODRIGUEZ

*"They say boys are made of snips and snails
and other things like puppy dog tails. But boy
moms can say straight from their hearts that
mostly they're just made of farts." ~Dude Mom*

My youngest son has always been different.

Quirky I guess is what you'd call him.

When he was one, he got attached to these puffy snow boots, they were short and blue and very Napoleon Dynamite-ish. He wore them straight through 2009. Even during summer, with shorts. No socks.

He had the smelliest one-year-old baby feet I've encountered in life. They made my ears burn they were so bad.

He transitioned from those into a pair of fireman rain boots one of our neighbors gave him.

He was always so proud of his preparedness when it rained, and he got to do a ridiculous amount of puddle jumping between the ages of two and three.

All of his quirks didn't manifest themselves fashionably. He had others too.

I remember once, I opened the toy box, and it was almost empty. Like I could see the bottom due to lack of toys. I wracked my brain for days about where those toys could be. I didn't look super hard for them or anything (secretly happy the giggling Elmo was MIA), but eventually

I discovered them as I was straightening the playroom. He'd packed everything that would fit into various backpacks.

For about a month, he labored to carry them everywhere with him. Even falling asleep on the floor with them strapped to his back.

I never figured out what inspired him to live that life, but I do know that he still appreciates an artfully packed bag.

When he got sick, his quirks sort of became ingrained into his being.

It was as though all of the kind of cute little things he used to do took over in his mind and became not-so-cute, frustrating tasks that he needed to complete.

We came to discover that that is just sort of what OCD is like when you're little.

You have all of these things your brain is telling you to do, and they're in there, no matter how much you try to ignore them, nudging, insisting, and pounding on your insides to break out. And then they do, and you feel better, but kind of worse because OMG DID ANYONE SEE THAT? I HOPE NO ONE SAW THAT. WHAT IF THEY MAKE FUN OF ME?!

His OCD is exasperated by a tic disorder which means he performs a lot of movements (everything from eye blinks to limping) and sounds (he's done throat clearing and humming) repetitively.

When it's overwhelming, he worries more about people noticing.

Because while he likes being different good, he doesn't want to be different bad. And he knows that people make that distinction.

He was diagnosed when he was four, and it has been a five-year struggle to get to where we are now.

It will continue to be a daily challenge, but he has gotten better about living with his disorder (I hate that word because it sounds like a bad thing, and while sometimes it is bad for him, it is also just a part of this person I love). He can control it better; he can manage it more effectively, he understands it better and, at times, he can even accept that it's a part of his life. His ability to do this (thanks to his weekly visits to his cognitive behavior therapist and more life changes than you can count on all of your appendages), makes it less pervasive, which in turn makes it again even easier for him to manage.

It's a vicious and beautiful circle that I wish he weren't in, but I also love being a part of.

We still have hard days, weeks, and months, but we also have amazing ones. Ones where I feel that even as I wish his life were easier, I also love who he has become. Ones where I realize that his different is the kind of different we should all want to be.

He worries more about things other kids don't even think about, like death, and old age, and the world, and its problems. He's more accepting of things others question. He's more open with his affection. And he lacks a filter that makes him honest but also endearing.

On the second day of second grade, he came down with his shirt on inside out and backward sparking a brief discussion...

Me: "Oh, so you're doing that? I didn't realize it was a school thing too." (He had been wearing them like this all summer long.)

Dude 3: "Yeah, I like it this way."

Me: "You know you will get a lot of questions, right?"

Dude 3: "Maybe, but I think it will be fine."

When he got home, he had his shirt changed –still inside out, but not also backward...

Me: "Oh, you changed?"

Dude 3: "I got tired of being questioned. Everyone thought I was confused, but really, it was them."

And he's right.

He gets himself; it's everyone else that can't keep up.

He's used to being the kink in the hose, the wrench in the plan, the *insert random other sayings used to describe the person who breaks the mold and bucks the status quo here*.

And his difference is both confusing and intriguing to those around him. He has a large personality accented by all of these special quirks that make him interesting and attractive and unique and even cool.

Which brings me to his socks.

THE GOLDEN NUGGET

S A B R I N A   G R E E R

"Never in my life did I think the words "stop
touching your brother's penis" would be something
that came out of my mouth daily!"~ Mom of Boys

*L*et me start by introducing myself. My name is Sabrina, but my friends refer to me as Sabs. I will assume if you are reading this that we are instant friends as members of the exclusive Mom of Boys Club, so please just call me Sabs.

In my past life, you know before the eternal bliss of parenthood was bestowed upon me, I was an International Fashion Model and self-taught but corporately paid Food & Beverage Consultant. Yes, you heard me correctly when I wasn't rubbing shoulders with celebs in Milan or gracing the pages of well-known catalogs I was getting generously paid to eat and drink all around the world…

I tell you this not to obnoxiously brag, but to give you a point of reference for later in this story. What was once a very spontaneous and exhilarating life has been replaced by something so much more (not sarcasm), and for the record, all the poo, farts and smelly feet in the world wouldn't change my mind or send me back. I have zero regrets and would not change a single thing in my current life.

I have three boys. The eldest recently turned eleven, my middle child (on so many levels) is two and a half, then the newest (and likely last) addition to our crazy clan is almost six months old. However, my motherhood journey only began five short years ago. You are probably either thinking that I am terrible at math or that mommy brain has taken over my mind. Fortunately (for me) you are wrong about both assumptions. My eldest was a ready-made AKA, my stepson. He lives with us full time, and although he did not inhabit my womb for forty weeks or leech from my breasts, as far as I am concerned you need both blood and water to survive, so I see him as nothing but my own.

As a boy mom, you have likely had numerous encounters with poop. Am I wrong? I didn't think so. From diaper explosions to potty training to presents being left behind in the bathtub, I have experienced it all. In hopes to get a few belly laughs out of you mamas, I am going to share a few of my poop filled adventures!

If you had asked me five years ago, as I was removing film-grade makeup off my face with a baby wipe if I could ever see myself wiping butts for a living, I would have laughed hysterically in your face. If you had asked as I was writing out wine tasting notes from a terrace in Napa Valley if I thought I would ever be writing a short story about poop for a parenting book, I would have peed my pants laughing at the idea. It is incredible how much can change in five years.

We are currently in the throes of potty training my toddler. He was doing quite well against all odds before we introduced his baby brother. At twenty-five months he was almost completely potty trained and then we rocked our little man's world and brought home a shriveled, noisy, diaper wearing, tiny human that took up a lot of mommy's time.

"Hmm, she is changing his diaper. Everyone thinks it is pretty cute when he poops in his pants. Mommy look, I can shit myself too!" I imagine says the sub-conscience mind of a jealous, confused, attention seeking toddler. Regression thus began and continues today six months later, although it is getting better.

I should mention for humor sake that my toddler is the size of a five-year-old. He is in five-year-old clothes, five-year-old pull-ups, and has five-year-old craps. He came out of my body at a whopping ten pounds and has been off the growth and development charts ever since. This kind of growth, albeit mostly genetic (daddy is tall) comes in combination with a massive appetite. I have a friend that requires daily updates on my son's food consumption so she can giggle about it with her fitness friends. So his poops are no longer cute.

There was one occasion when he thought that it would be fun to paint with his feces. Yes, I said paint. He was grabbing handfuls of his human waste to make drawings on his walls and bed sheets. He was quite proud of his art. These are the times that I find parenting to be the most challenging. It is hard to know how to respond to things like that. Luckily, I studied psychology at the university, so the right answer exists in the bowels (ha ha) of my long term memory. This has not been a reoccurring incident, thank goodness.

We are not a religious family, but we do celebrate Easter. This past Easter corresponded with my eldest sons eleventh birthday, so the entire, extremely long, five day weekend became a multilevel celebration. We spent many hours traveling in the car, which with all boys becomes a fart-box (like a hotbox of disgusting stink) and visiting lots of family. I think with three children it should be mandatory for all family to come to you because it is a pain to pack the potty seat, diapers, wipes, and adequate clothing changes. Somehow though, we always seem to be the ones doing the visiting.

We found ourselves at one grandparent's place, after several days at the others. The toddler hadn't pooped in twenty-four hours. Minutes before we sat down to a home cooked family meal he said, "Mommy, I need to go poo on the potty." "What? You are kidding me child?" I thought to myself. We did not have his potty seat, and we were in someone else's home about to sit down to dinner. I was nursing the baby to try and keep him quiet for the duration of a meal, so I told my husband to take him to the toilet. Honestly, I assumed it was a false alarm.

Screams of joy and excitement bellowed from the powder room that was attached to the dining room where we were about to sit and eat. They were followed by my husband yelling "you have to come see this!!" I found myself thinking "did he poop out a piece of Lego or something, oh no what did he eat, what's the big deal here?" Next thing you know our entire family (I mean everyone in the house not just our immediate weirdos) are surrounding the toilet in awe as if this kid just pooped out a shiny gold nugget. I look down, not to see gold but the longest, widest, and all around biggest turd that I have ever seen in my life. Yes, it was a turd. A turd disguised as a gold nugget because the pride and excitement on that little boys face followed by the family celebration that occurred is as priceless as it gets.

I will close this story by sharing my gratitude to the universe that a turd now gives me the same pleasure and excitement that only a Michelin Star restaurant or a free trip on a private charter yacht once would have!

IMAGINED DIALOGUES BETWEEN MY SONS

KATIA BISHOPS

"I'm sorry we're an hour late. My four-year-old was trying to listen to his ear." ~Iamthemilk

SUMMER 2012 – FIRST MEETING

*B*ig brother (3 years old): Hey, welcome to the world. Nice but boring to meet you. Your role in this life henceforth is Sidekick. No offense, but you look under-qualified. Lucky for you, I offer mentorship.

So, you know how when boys like girls they pull on their pigtails or ignore their calls? The equivalent of that in the parent/child world is *don't let them sleep*. That's how they'll know you like them. Got it?

Little brother (newborn) spits up

Big brother: I'll take that as a 'yes.'

SOMETIME IN 2013

Big brother (4 years old): You get an A (adequate) for your performance so far, but I still think we need a system. I don't always want to wake up at 5 am, I mean of course I do (!), but what if I feel like sleeping in one morning? Someone has to cover the 5-6am shift.

Whispers

Remember: for reasons no one but us will ever know; it's essential that this household is up and running by 5 am, 'by' being the operative term here.

Mysterious form of sealing the deal ensues. Might involve peeing outside the toilet

STILL IN 2013

Big brother (4 years old): So what being a boy means to me - and therefore to you - these days is using the word poop all the time. Remember: poop is a complete sentence. Oh, hey, Tough Crowd, I said poop...

Little brother (1-year-old): ...

Big brother: Whatever, you'll get it when you're four.

SPRING 2014

Big brother (5 years old): I'll have you initial and sign this waiver since I'm about to share classified information with you and I don't know how waivers work.

* Little brother empties out a box of Kleenex and tries to wear it on his head*

Am I mature beyond my years? Affirmative. Did I ace emotional intelligence? Killed it. Is my middle name empathy? In most circles. Don't let my reputation dazzle you. I keep a dark secret. I kill bugs for no apparent reason.

Little brother: I know. You do this on our walks and in the backyard and mom always tries to appeal to your inner Buddhist, but it never works.

Big brother *ignores him*: So would your dark passenger like to join mine?

Little brother: O Captain! My Captain!

2015

Big brother (6 years old): I'm going to share a few rules of thumb with you: Always be spilling; dress code: clothing optional; downtime who?

Little brother (3 years old) *appears from behind the living room curtain, naked in a winter hat, sunglasses and one sock *: Way ahead of you.

Together: BWAHAHAHA!

2016

Big brother (7 years old): Remember how back when I was four I used to say 'poop' all the time?

Little brother (4 years old): You said *poop*! HAHAHA HAHAHA!!!!!!!

* Big brother yells at the top of his lungs* AAAAAAAAAHHHH HHHHHHHH!!!!!! AAAAAAAAAAAHHHHHHHH!!!!!!! Now I just do this instead. This is how I self-express and communicate the same message: maturity, independence, sense of humor. This is what young men who don't need to listen to their mommy about wearing snow pants sound like. AAAAAAAAAHHHHHHHHHHH!!!! It also works with other things; you can just yell them out. Try it!

Little brother: AAAAAAAAAAAAAHHHHHHHHHH!!! Yell them out. Try it!!

Big brother: No, you don't have to repeat that part.

Little brother: No, you don't have to repeat that part.

EARLY 2017

> Dear little brother,
>
> It's me, big brother. Some things are too risky to be communicated verbally, so I'm writing this letter instead. By the way, this letter will self-destruct when I'm done reading it to you because you can't read, and

by self-destruct I mean: you, me and some PG rated kitchen appliances. Don't worry about it; there's a parent-friendly code for what we're about to do: science experiment.

Please use the following checklist daily to defend the title Sidekick:

- Ask yourself: do all my pants have a little pencil-size hole in them on the thigh area?
- Have I performed any science experiments today?
- Have I facilitated any deep breathing sessions for my mother today (deep breathing being a euphemism for horrified gasps)?
- Do my parents look like they're slacking off (scan their surroundings for hot beverages, books or - in especially naïve moments - plates with food)? If you've answered 'yes' to this, please consider introducing a two, three or four-wheel mode of transportation to your domestic environment. Remember: helmets are considered outerwear.

The indicators of successful performance on your part will require checking your parents for:

- Double bagging- are your parents currently in possession of a single set of eye bags? If you answered yes to this then you're not living up to your potential. Any old person can get eye bags. It takes your children's dedication and commitment to diversifying your sleep routine for your eye bags to grow a second pair.
- Can their posture be likened to that of a turtle? A slight tilt of the head and misalignment of the spine speak volumes of the work you've been doing over the years pushing them to the edges of their beds, demanding to be carried around.
- At home, do they need to change their socks six times a day because wet? Congratulations, you really get it.

Well done, little brother, carry on (but none of that "keep calm" nonsense).

LIFE WITH TWO BOYS

KARSSON HEVIA

*"Life with Boys teaches you to fear the silence-
not the chaos... the lack of sound is much
more frightening"~Too Many Open Tabs*

I have to be honest; during the brief, yet blissful interim after getting married and before my husband and I decided we wanted to actively start trying for a baby and join the ranks of the ever elusive *parenthood*, I, like many women, loved fantasizing about what our children would look like. Would she have my eyes and my husband's hair? Or maybe my olive skin and his freckles. My daily conjuring of daydreaming images always looked the same; a beautiful baby girl whose rosy cheeks and tiny blond tendrils would light up the entire room as she smiled. She'd wear bows in her tousled hair and be dressed in the cutest floral rompers and ballet pink moccasins, all the while quietly bouncing along like a little floral fairy, her doll trailing behind her. We'd play Barbies, and dig in the sandbox and read books together while she sat in my lap and helped turn the pages. These images seemed to closely mirror those experiences from my childhood and were reminiscent of the relationship I had with my mother growing up. After all, that's all I knew. I came from an overly female-dominated family where boys were somewhat absent. I knew girl stuff. Pretty pink, lacy, smelly-good, girl stuff. Then the day came that we found out we were having a boy.

It was like a cruel joke put on by the universe. After 27 years of speaking all things girl, I suddenly was forced to learn a foreign language. How could I possibly decorate a nursery when all I'd Pinterested for the last two years were pictures of light pink French provincial dressers and antique crystal-cut chandeliers? And how could I be expected to *name* said baby when my short, yet coveted list of baby names solely included those of delicate and feminine throwback names that paid homage to the beautiful women of yesteryears? *'This was simply not going to work'* I thought to myself, my utter disbelief being too grave to conceal from my husband, who celebrated ecstatically, by the way, the day we found out the gender. I was left in absolute shock.

Fast-forward five and a half years later, and I am currently the happy mom of two little dudes— complete with blond tendrils framing their darling faces. Their rosy cheeks giving way to sets of dimples that, you guessed it, light up a room. They love deeply with their whole heart and each showcase diverse, yet strong personalities. They live with great conviction, one balancing out the other. Together, they enrich my life in ways I never thought imaginable, and I'm honored to be the one who they call 'mom.' While there are definitely no bows to add to their sun-kissed locks, or afternoons spent dressing up Barbies, and no ballet-anything —surprisingly — this still doesn't remain the most poignant detail that differentiates reality from my earlier childless musings. The single biggest difference between the two? The fact that life is anything but *quiet.*

Calm moments don't have a residence in our world. So much so, that even those seemingly *quiet* activities don't stand a chance at a peaceful presence. Take for example, play-dough. A rather innocuous game that for all intents and purposes should elicit a relaxed state of play. Nope. Not a chance. It evolves into a wild raucous of one-upping, play-dough-eating, multicolored weaponry by which each child ends up somehow injured. Or how about Legos. Another game by which no sound or physical contact is necessary, yet like the old saying goes, where there's a will, there's a way, and boy (no pun, intended), and do these kiddos have will.

I always find it especially eye-opening just how different boys are from girls after an afternoon play date spent with one of my girlfriends who have girls. The stark, innate difference in their behaviors is truly astounding. Girls look objectively at objects, analyzing how they can be of fun to them. Boys look to see how they can be dismantled and disseminated. Girls like to line toys up and bring like objects together. Boys, too, like to group items, particularly in an effort to ram things into one another, creating a chain reaction of destruction. Now, don't get me wrong, it's absolutely not that one is bad, and the other is good- it's just that boys thrive on a completely different subset of internal motivators, most of which are derived from sound decimal and parts smashing.

When I think about my daily life with boys, there are a few inherent truisms that come to mind. I've never once started a sentence with, 'So the boys were quietly _____.' Nor have I ever thought to myself, 'Wow that was a quiet afternoon!' Or better yet, I've become so used to repeating myself at least three times about most everything because as much as they like to talk, listening seems to completely elude them. But you see, as a mom of two boys, quiet is not what you wish for because when boys are quiet, it means that shit is about to go down. When they're quiet, it's because they're surreptitiously eating an ice cream sandwich at 7:30 in the morning outside in the backyard behind a tree. It's because they've decided to go into the garage and rummage through the garden tools, swinging iron rakes dangerously in the air, 2 cm from each other's head within the three minutes it took you to take a shower. Or, it could absolutely be part and parcel to the fact that they've decided to make a tasting menu of all the ChapSticks from our bathroom cabinet in an effort to determine which is more delectable. Quiet quite simply equates disaster in a household of boys.

Life with two boys, ages 2.5 years-old and 5.5 years-old, most definitely isn't easy. This time in our lives somewhat resembles that of anxiously watching a smoldering, volatile volcano; we know at any minute, things are more than likely, about to erupt. Down time is few-and-far-between and their energy and intensity is always kicked into high-gear. Most days come to a close with my ears ringing and my body longing for some much-needed rest and relaxation, yet, what I lack in quiet moments, I more than make up for with the biggest, loudest, love that a mom could ever ask for. They love me to the moon and back, and on most days, it sounds like they're en route.

A Beautiful Heart

Bianca Jamotte LeRoux

"I just Googled 'My toddler plays with his poop, normal?' So, how's your day?" – Real Mommy Confessions

*E*very story about the strength of the love between a mom and her son is true.

My son is the man of my dreams. He has deep brown eyes that turn golden or green, depending on his mood (just like mine); his hair is dark with sun-kissed highlights, like mine used to be. Our skin and freckles are the same color, so much so that he would rest his tiny hand on my chest while breastfeeding and I would marvel at how I could barely decipher where I ended, and he began.

Casey's entrance into the world was intense and theatrical, and I adored him immediately. My son popped out violently, one hand beside his head, screaming and pissing on the doctors and nurses. His thick hair stood straight up on top of his head in a perfect 80s-style Mohawk, and he kicked and shrieked angrily until he ran out of breath and turned purple. I could barely get a word out after his birth because I was laughing, and crying tears of joy. When I finally caught my breath, I said to my husband in between gasps, "He's a rock star." My little drama king continued to scream bloody murder until he was placed on my breast, where he remained for the next 15 months. Even after he weaned, I was still his "lovie" and source of comfort.

He preferred me to any other human on the planet, which I complained about but secretly loved. He wanted me and only me. He would scream if anyone else held him, cry if others sang to him, and would sleep only when he was on my chest. Initially, I chalked up his finicky nature to the fact that he was a momma's boy, but as he grew, so did his temper when he didn't get his way. Casey's outbursts became a running joke to our friends and loved ones. I would share pictures of his "craziness" and "battiness" with captions such as "I wouldn't let him play with the garbage," or "I took away the fork he threw at me." I poked fun at everything, but in reality, I was at my wits' end.

But even as I made light of the situation, I had doubts. Was he a brat and I couldn't face it because he was my baby? I knew Casey was a tender and loving boy. He gave the best hugs and kisses. He looked at me like a goddess when I sang to him; his laugh made even the grumpiest old men at restaurants smile. Was I the only person who would ever witness his beautiful heart?

Over the years, his tactics changed, but Casey's temper stayed the same. By the time he started school, his teachers had noticed something that I had also been worried about: Casey seemed to have "sensory issues." Each day when he walked into his classroom and greeted his teachers, he would hide behind me and twiddle his fingers until he found a toy he liked. He would cling to that toy for the rest of the day. His teachers informed me that some noises had him clutching his ears, and he would yell at the other kids to stop singing during music lessons. Transitioning from one activity to the next would throw him off-balance, so much so that he would scream and hit his teachers. They asked if he was like this at home, or if, maybe, he wasn't ready for school. I searched my brain for a joke, some way to ease the tightness in my chest, but I had nothing. I told them this was my son, always, unless he was alone with me.

One day, after a particularly difficult drop-off, I sat in my car, fearing the worst. I made a list of everything the teachers had observed and the issues I had with him at home: the tantrums, his quick and sometimes violent temper, the difficulty getting him to do something as simple as getting dressed. I read everything I could online and asked questions in mom groups. With all the information I could gather on my own, I scheduled a check-up with the pediatrician and braced myself for answers. I knew that we would face head on whatever was going on with my little man and get him the help he needed, but I didn't yet know what I was dealing with. The one piece of information I held onto that gave me hope was that he was very aware of how people felt around him and how his actions affected them. No matter what I learned about him that day, Casey showed compassion and tenderness to others. His beautiful heart counted for something.

Our pediatrician, as politely as possible, dismissed my concerns. "He's exactly like my oldest. I'm not saying he won't always be a bit tough to deal with—trust me, he will be—but he's fine, and you shouldn't worry."

I tucked her advice in the back of my brain and repeated it to myself as I dragged my son to see an ENT—not because I thought he could help me decipher what was going on with my son emotionally, but to address the six ear infections Casey had suffered over the winter.

After a routine check-up, which we survived with minimal screaming and fighting, we were sent down the hall to have his hearing tested. My stomach dropped as we walked into the tiny room and saw the dimly lit soundproof booth, but the technician just smiled, knelt down and calmly spoke to my son.

"Do you like animals?" she asked. Casey peaked out from behind my legs and nodded. "Good, because you get to hear them speak to you in these headphones. You'll hear birds chirping, and dogs barking."

"Sharks?" Casey asked.

"No, no sharks, but there might be some monkeys in there." Still kneeling, she looked up at me and winked. As my son slipped the too-large headphones onto his little head and stepped into the booth, he excitedly rattled off information about sharks and dinosaurs.

He finished the test with no problems. As we stepped out of the booth, the technician asked me if Casey had a good ear for music. She could tell by how he related to the sounds in the headphones, even with the fluid in his ears; he had perfect hearing.

I don't know why this was the piece of information that lifted the cloud over my heart, but somehow I could tell that this woman saw my boy at his core, and she understood him immediately. This set my spirit at ease, to see someone else able to connect with him so simply.

I learned a lot that day, but most importantly that Casey is not sick. He doesn't have a learning disability. Casey isn't a jerk, he isn't a brat, and he doesn't need to "man up." The only thing "wrong" with Casey is that his emotions are raw and on the surface. I love this about him; I think it's something we lose as we grow up. A lot of what makes him a difficult child are traits that I know will make him an incredible man. He's thoughtful and sensitive, but he's not a pushover. He's empathetic and takes people's feelings to heart, especially the people he loves.

As he gets older, he'll encounter people who will continue to tell him he's "too sensitive"; he won't be able to avoid them. He'll gradually learn to hide all of this from the world. He'll have to protect himself and his emotions from a society that doesn't understand him. It is only in childhood, in his mother's arms, that he is safe enough to experience life the way he does now. So I will nurture my son for as long as I can. It won't be long before he hides this side of himself, even from me.

Through all of this, as I have grown to understand my son, I have fallen even more in love with him. He is now four years old and can fully articulate his feelings. He lets me know that his socks feel yucky when the seam is not in the right place. He doesn't feel comfortable in certain clothes and wants to wear what he calls "ordinary clothes." He doesn't like the "noise" the other kids make during music time at school, but with that comes his beautiful heart. He is moved to tears by beautiful music; he paints because it makes him "feel calm." He wakes me in the middle of the night to make sure I know he loves me.

One night last winter, Casey, my daughter, and I snuggled up on the sofa to watch a Christmas movie before bed. My son sat quietly, tucked into my side. As the music swelled over the credits and the TV glowed with Christmas lights, I heard quiet sniffles coming from the little man snuggled under my arm. "Buddy, what's the matter?" I asked him.

I pulled him onto my lap so we could talk face-to-face. His mouth was turned down, his big brown eyes were dark and deep, and big tears rolled down his cheeks. "It's so beautiful it makes me sad, and so, so happy." As I held my little man in my arms, and he heaved all of his feelings into my chest, it was then that I knew I wouldn't have to worry. I love that he is a drama king.

And I know, when he is ready, he will show
his beautiful heart to the world.

When Dinner Conversations Get a Little Bit Shady

By Jennifer Bairos

"My son is at that adorable age where he believes everything we tell him. Like that sometimes we only have 'grown up chocolate' in the house" ~A Splendid Messy Life.

There are many milestones we think about as new parents. We are so attentive and aware when it comes to things like sleeping through the night, first foods, first words, first steps, or the first day of daycare. We read parenting books and blogs regularly, and we follow our children's progress with those BabyCentre emails. We are proud and excited at each milestone reached, and we happily share all of these big events and anecdotes with our friends and family. Photographs are taken. Grandparents are called. Baby books are filled out, or, at the very least, we think about filling them out.

But one milestone they don't really prepare you for in all of those baby books is the first time your son asks about what girls look like naked. I suppose there probably *are* books about how to talk to young boys about this topic, but clearly, none that I have gotten around to reading.

Now, my husband, Rob, and I always knew this conversation would come up at some point; however, we had no concept of at what point along the timeline of parenthood it would appear, so when our son started asking us these questions it took us by surprise.

Let me set the scene.

One evening, Rob and I were having dinner with our four-year-old son, Sebastian. Rob started clearing the dishes and headed into the kitchen. Sebastian and I stayed at the table while he was finishing up (because those veggies don't eat themselves), and then this conversation began:

Sebastian – It was Molly's* mommy's birthday today.

Me – That's fun! Do you know who has a birthday on Friday?

Sebastian – Who?

Me – Dani *(One of my friends he sees a few times a week.)*

Sebastian – What will she do?

Me – She's going to the movies.

Sebastian – What movie is she seeing?

Me – It's called *50 Shades Darker.*

Sebastian – What is it about?

Me – A boy and a girl who like each other.

Sebastian – Who is the villain? *(Sebastian happens to be particularly obsessed with villains right now.)*

Me – Another girl who doesn't want them to be friends.

(Slight pause)

Sebastian – What does a vagina look like?

At that point, Rob, who had heard the entire conversation, came out of the kitchen, and he and I both exchanged this look that was a combination of "OK, I guess we're doing this now" and "OMG. He doesn't *really* know what *50 Shades Darker* is, right?"

Previously, Sebastian knew that boys have penises and girls have vaginas, but we hadn't had any other conversations beyond that.

I suppose I probably shouldn't have thrown in the part about *50 Shades Darker*, but that really *was* the movie my friend was going to see on her birthday, and I didn't feel like making something else up. Also, I'm fairly certain that on this day that any movie with a boy and a girl in the plotline would have led to Sebastian's question.

My actual reply to Sebastian was something like this: "You know what, honey that is a great question. How about I find a picture to show you this week?" Thankfully, he seemed satisfied with this plan.

Then, I immediately texted a transcript of the conversation I had with Sebastian to my friend, Dani. She doesn't have kids yet, but I knew this whole situation would make her laugh until she cried. I wasn't wrong.

After Sebastian fell asleep that night, I sat in front of my laptop. I didn't want to Google anything that combined the words *naked*, *children*, or *vagina*, so I went to where I solve most of my problems: Amazon Prime.

Even on Amazon, my search terms were very carefully crafted. I went with "*best books for teaching preschoolers about body parts.*"

After browsing through a few different options, I decided to go with *The Bare Naked Book* by Kathy Stinson and *Amazing You!* by Gail Saltz. Fortunately, my local library carried both of these titles, so I was able to place them on hold, and they arrived a few days later.

Sebastian loves the library, especially when we request books that are put on hold just for him. We went to pick the books up after school one afternoon, and then we came home, sat on the couch and started to read. We read *The Bare Naked Book*, he saw the picture he was looking for, and that was that. He acknowledged it, accepted it, then carried on his way and began playing with his other toys. His question had been answered. We never even opened the second book.

During parent-teacher interviews that week I had an awkward conversation with his kindergarten teacher and told her that Sebastian had been asking these questions at home, and we had been trying to answer them. I explained as well that we'd told him he couldn't talk about these things with his friends at school. His teacher was very kind, and she assured us that every year at some point the 4 and 5-year-olds always go through a phase where they are very interested in everyone's body parts for about a month, and then they move on to something else, so these questions were expected around now.

A few weeks later, I was negotiating with Sebastian which books he needed to return to the library (because while he loves borrowing books *from* the library, he still hasn't fully grasped the concept that we also need to eventually return books *to* the library). He was carefully guarding his current favorite I Spy books (renewed three times and soon to be overdue). Instead, he offered, "I'm done with the vagina books, Mommy!"

Sebastian hasn't asked about or mentioned the topic since then. What I think I've learned from all of this is that these conversations might feel like a bigger deal for us than they are for them. In a time when discussions about respect for bodies and gender is at an all time high, it is so important for us as parents to create a space for these questions to be comfortable and permitted. Gender can be complicated, and this is certainly not going to be the last conversation we have with Sebastian about bodies. More than likely there will be more questions that again stop us in our tracks. However, my husband and I are fully aware that how we talk with Sebastian about girls' bodies now will influence how he looks at women moving forward. Our hope is that he continues to ask us as many questions as he wants for as long as possible, even when they come at us during dinner.

*name has been changed

You're My Best

RACHAEL BOLEY

"...And the 'Worst Mother of The Year' award goes to me! Why you ask? Oh, obviously because I wouldn't allow my son to wear the dirty red shorts he pulled out of the laundry basket that he wore for the last two days." ~ Three Boys and a Mom

I always knew I wanted to be a mother. I was a typical little girl pushing around strollers and carrying baby dolls in swaddles. I had a book where I kept a list of names I loved and considered for my future children. When I pictured motherhood, I always imagined I'd have a little girl. It's not that I didn't want to have boys; I just always pictured some pink in my life.

I have learned over the course of time that the best way to make God laugh is to tell him your plans.

I found out I was pregnant with twins at my twenty-week ultrasound. I'd had an ultrasound to confirm pregnancy around seven weeks, and they said, "Congratulations! You've got one healthy baby in there." I went about the next thirteen weeks as usual. Well, as usual as it gets for first-time pregnancy. I showed up to my twenty-week appointment all a flutter, and I couldn't wait to see what that one healthy baby was going to be. Pink or blue? Boy or girl? Penis or vagina? Farts or Barbies? (Not that any of that is exclusive to one sex or the other, but you get what I'm saying.)

Imagine my surprise when as I'm lying there the ultrasound techni-cian says, "Well, they're both head down, so that's good!"

Excuse me…BOTH!!??!?!?

I looked over and low and behold, two heads on the screen. It's a good thing I was already laying down because my little pregnant knees were buckling. I thought this was some sort of sick ultrasound humor and it took me several minutes to process that she was in no way joking.

There were, in fact, two babies inside my body.

There was a time not long before that day that I didn't think I could get pregnant at all. I'd spent years destroying my body with a near deadly eating disorder, and I had lost hope that motherhood was in the cards for me. I lost hope that my body could carry a baby, and I'd lost confidence in my capacity to be a good mother. Finding out I was pregnant was monumental for me in more ways than one. Finding out twenty weeks into the pregnancy that there were two of them, was colossal.

It felt like reckless grace from heaven and I still at times struggle to process the gift of it.

As she searched my uterus, she finally found what we were looking for. Two boy parts confirming I was about to not only become a mom, but I was going to become a mom of two identical boys.

That was one of the best days of my life.

When I became pregnant with my third child, I was sure it was go-ing to be a girl. My pregnancies were entirely different, and I just knew that the little girl I'd always imagined was showing up as my third child.

Well, wrong again. My blue world was destined to stay exponen-tially blue.

Never in my life did I expect to become a single mom of three boys. That wasn't written in my book of plans when I was a little girl. But I have learned that when we think we're at the end, we are standing at the beginning of everything.

I have learned to take the endings, the shattering's, and the unrav-eling's of my life and use them to propel me into my purpose. My boys have taught me more about life and myself than I may ever teach them, but the beauty is in the journey we get to walk together.

My boys are my tribe, and I am theirs.

I have many things I say to my sons every day. Things I have said since they were born. Things like, "I love you to the moon and back," "We're a team," and "You guys are the best." There's more of course. Things like, "Please don't sit on your brother's face," "Toothbrushes are for teeth, not penises," and "Say excuse me." But I digress.

As they developed their speech and began saying things back to me, they'd repeat what I said to them. One day when I was driving home from daycare, my son said in the sweetest voice from the back, "Mom, you're my best."

It stuck, and that's a saying we say all the time now.

"You're my best."

As I've thought about it, I realize more and more how true it is.

As mothers, we give our all and a little bit more to our babies and families. We give them the best we have; even on the days it doesn't feel good enough. We let them eat first. We abandon our freedom. We surrender the ability to shower or pee in peace. We give up sleep and all of our time. We find ways not to say the things we think in our sleep deprived state and instead pour out our love. We do what needs to be done for our babies, whether we feel like it or not at that moment. We give them our best. Day in and day out, they are a manifestation of our very best.

As mothers who give so much, we often simultaneously feel like we aren't giving, doing, or being enough. There is always something we feel we missed. Something we wish we'd done differently. Some way we feel we should have given more.

What I have learned through my boys, motherhood, and life, in general, is that we are enough.

When we feel weak, we still do what needs to be done.

When we are sick, we still take care of our babies.

When we are tired, we keep going.

When we fall, we get back up.

That's enough. That's more than enough. That's our best.

So when I say to my boys, "You're my best," I mean that with every fiber of my being. They are the best thing I've ever done. They are the reason I show up every day as my best. They are all that exists within me and a whole lot more.

When they say to me, "Mom, you're my best," they mean that. They don't mean, "You're my best only on the days you get it right." They mean, "You're my best, you're my everything, all the time, no matter what."

That's what motherhood is to me. It's the best of everything. The best of my failure. The best of my success. The best of my effort. The best of my energy. The best of my pain. The best of my experience. The best of my time. The best of my life. The best of me.

Almost nothing about much of my life has gone the way I planned, and I thank God for that every single day. In spite of my plans and all my mistakes, my boys showed up and made me their best.

Boy Mom 101

Mikenzie Oldham

"You know you're a boy mom when you hear your kid randomly say "smell my butt," and you are not surprised." ~Me & All My Boys

What have I learned from being a boy mom? Boys give new meaning and new life to a Momma's soul. When a baby boy is born, EVERYTHING changes. The person I thought I was before having boys is drastically different from the person that I am now. I am a stronger, more compassionate, and a more patient person with a much higher sense of self-worth.

Boys can bring out the best and the worst in their Mamas. We've all had hard days when you are running late, and one kid pushes the other kid in the mud; the breakfast burned because you were breaking up a boy fight, and you've spent more time searching for a missing shoe than dressing yourself. But the good days far outweigh the bad ones in the eyes of those boys.

Little boys have a way of bringing out their Momma's tomboy side, her silly side, and her courageous side. Boys push their Momma's to her furthest limit and then find a way to push some more before they smother her with hugs and kisses. Boys are the silent strength behind every great "boy mom."

When people ask if we will "try for a girl" or if we wished "one was a girl"... the answer is NO! I wouldn't know how to raise a girl. What do they do with all those bows and Barbies and how do you get their hair in pigtails? These are the exact two human beings that were meant to be in our life. I was destined to be a "boy mom," and I wouldn't have it any other way.

So can I describe life with boys in a nutshell? Boys are wild, rowdy and super stinky. Boys like to wear their favorite Batman T-shirt and basketball shorts every single day. Boys leave Lego parts strategically placed on the floor like little land mines. Boys wrestle, pick, poke, tap, trip and tackle each other all day long. From "Son up until son down" they do extremely crazy things that make you panic. Boys think it is ok to burp louder than their brother in public places. Boys think poop is a noun, an adjective, and a prefix. Before these two boys, I was too embarrassed to even say the word poop.

Before I had my sons, I had NO clue what a transformer was, and now I know all of their names. A rumble was something the greasers did in Grease, and now it's a daily activity in my house. I never realized that you could actually tickle someone else until they pee their pants. I didn't understand just how much boys love super heroes or how much boys eat. (I still don't understand where it all goes?)

Before these two boys, I never knew I would be lucky enough to be not one, but two little boys first love. I am a proud momma to two little boys and will gladly wash the Batman shirt every single night, make jokes about the dogs stinky toots, lay on the floor while two little boys attack me for a tickle fight, transform something with my eyes closed, hold a worm for my son while he finds a cup to put it in, chug a drink so we can have a burping contest in the middle of a nice restaurant, or put a Band-aide on someone's owie after they have jumped out of a tree like a daredevil.

I am a boy mom. I am a proud supporter of dressing as super heroes to go the grocery store or leaving the kitchen a mess so that we can have a nerf gun war down the hall. Moms are led to believe that WE are the ones teaching them. But little boys teach us everything. They teach us what is important and what to believe in.

I have developed a new level of patience. I don't get annoyed when my boys search for the perfect beetle to catch or when they ransack the house looking for a lost shoe (I swear he had it on five minutes ago).

I have developed a new level of compassion to use when one of them brings a baby mouse up to the patio and begs me to let them keep it. I have a new found sense of courage. There are moments when I feel like a momma bear protecting her cubs. I have developed a gut instinct, a mother's intuition, and a primal territorial love. The mother son bond is special. Little boys tell their Momma's they are beautiful. Between arguing with their brother and nose diving off the back steps, they will stop to pick their momma a flower and thank her for being "so cool."

I thought I knew how to be a mom. I thought I knew what was truly important in life. Until they came along and changed everything. They've taught me what unconditional love truly is.

MOMMY TRIAGE

SARAH E. WESTFALL

*"You know you're a boy mom when your feet have
developed LEGO-shaped callouses." ~Life in Blue*

*W*hen I became a mom, I had no idea I was signing up to work in crisis management. A cook? Sure. A teacher? You bet. But never did I think that daily life would require fewer snuggles and more emergency response.

But here I am, four boys under the age of eight and feeling like a paramedic, psychologist, and firefighter all wrapped into one.

Most days, my job is simply keeping the littles alive...out of the neighbor's beehives, away from the stairs, or next to me at the store. I block rocks from being thrown at babies and stop toddlers from swallowing LEGOs. I don't sit down unless I'm nursing the baby, and sometimes not even then.

The crises generally happen one at a time, in rapid succession. But once in a full moon (okay more like once a week), the chaos occurs all at once. I call it mommy triage, and it looks a little like this:

Our youngest was only two weeks old, and I was just beginning to get my feet wet in the world of having four kids. It was late afternoon, and our oldest was due off the bus in minutes. Because he was a first grader, I was required to meet him at the bus stop. I only had to walk to the end of our driveway, but that fifty-foot hike felt like a mile when I had a four-year-old, sixteen-month-old, and newborn in tow. Each bus stop took careful planning.

That particular day, the newborn was asleep in the infant swing but was starting to get hungry. He squirmed and fussed mildly, so I ran to the kitchen to put on my shoes. I planned to nurse quickly and then run out to meet the bus.

I was gone only a moment when I heard my toddler start to cry. It was the kind of cry that makes a mother's heart stop. I knew instantly that he was hurt, so I rushed back into the living room to see what was wrong. I picked him up off the floor and was shocked to see a golf-ball size lump protruding from his forehead.

Panic rose immediately, and my throat closed up. My mind swirled with what I should do next: *Do I call the doctor? Go to the emergency room? Find the ibuprofen? Get a bag of ice? Ice! Yes, that was what I needed to do next.*

With the toddler in arms, I hurried to the kitchen to grab an ice pack for his swollen head. But it was a no-go. The more I tried to ice his wound, which looked purple and red and about to burst, the more he thrashed around. The ice wasn't happening.

Meanwhile, the baby started to cry. He was hungry and not having it.

Cue the four-year-old. Either unaware or not fazed by the crying of his two younger brothers, he began to whine: "Mom! I'm hungry. I need a snack!" I didn't respond to him immediately, so the whining got louder and more drawn out. "MOM! I'm huuuuuuuuungry!"

The toddler continued to scream and throw back his head. Nothing I did would soothe him, which only made me panic more. So I called my husband.

Ben answered and was greeted by the sounds of weeping and gnashing of teeth.

My words came out in a jumble: "Jamisonfellandhithishead."

"Wait, what?"

I did my best to slow down and explain, "I'm pretty sure Jamison ran into the cinder block wall in the living room. A huge lump appeared on his forehead immediately, and I don't know what to do because he won't let me put ice on it. It's huge. I don't know how it didn't split open. I'm afraid he's going to have a concussion. What do I do?"

Ben tried to offer some advice and encouragement, but I honestly stopped hearing him at that moment. I had two wailing kids and one who was convinced he just might die of hunger. I glanced at the clock. I had five minutes until the bus arrived.

"Okay, I'm going to figure this out. I'll just keep you posted." I hung up the phone and took a deep breath. "I can do this."

I put the wounded toddler on the couch while texting a picture of his forehead to my brother, also an orthopedic surgeon. I ran to grab the inconsolable baby out of swing while informing the preschooler that he "just needed to wait because mama was dealing with an emergency." I probably didn't say it so politely.

Without hesitation, I ran to the TV and popped a Baby Einstein video into the DVD player. Almost instantly, the four-year-old and the toddler quieted. Pictures of trains and tiger puppets to a Vivaldi soundtrack was apparently enough to distract them from their current woes.

I sat down on the couch in between them with the baby in my arms. From that vantage point, I could keep an eye on the head injury, nurse the baby, keep the preschooler occupied, and watch for the impending bus from the window.

Just as quickly as the chaos had started, everything quieted down. Within minutes, I had a baby with a full belly, and all I could hear was the sound of classical music coming from the TV. I texted my husband an "all is well" to let him know we weren't hospital bound. I was even able to walk to the end of the driveway just in time to see my first grader jump off the bus.

I went back inside and placed the now-sleeping baby back in his swing. The first grader sat down next to his brothers on the couch, instantly sucked in by the hypnotic force that is Baby Einstein. A quick check of the toddler revealed a less severe-looking lump and a smile on his face. No signs of a concussion. I took a deep sigh of relief and went to get my boys some microwave popcorn.

As a mom of all boys, you take advantage of a quiet moment when you find it. So as the popcorn popped, I slumped over on the kitchen counter to catch my breath and reach for my chocolate stash. I felt like a soldier who had just returned from the front lines.

What just happened? I replayed the madness of the last fifteen minutes in my brain and popped a couple dozen Reese's Pieces in my mouth. Keeping my boys safe was obviously part of the mom gig, but it wasn't as simple as I once thought it would be.

A Girl Mom on Becoming a Boy Mom

Glynis Ratcliffe

"When the most exciting part of your
drive is spotting a garbage truck, that's
life with a boy!" ~ Glynis Ratcliffe

*W*hen I found out I was having a boy, I have to admit: I was terrified. With a teenaged stepdaughter and a preschool-aged biological daughter, I had gotten used to parenting girls, and my girls were relatively worry-free, in many ways. And, if you think about it, there are a million rumors about all the crazy things that go along with having boys.

I have a friend whose little boy peed down the air intake vent, while he was potty training, and was incredibly proud of himself for his aim.

I worked at a health food store where, in the baby department, they sold something for baby boys called the "Pee Pee Teepee" to protect parents from being inadvertently sprayed while changing a diaper.

I have another friend whose little boy decided that smearing his poop on the walls was the ideal way to communicate his frustration at no longer wearing diapers.

I have yet another friend whose son has had one hand attached to his penis since the day he was born, which is kind of a problem, given the fact that he's now eight years old.

I'm not exaggerating, not even a little.

I still remember friends with two boys of their own having us over for dinner one time, when I was pregnant with our first, though we didn't yet know the gender. They were hoping to show us how great it was to have little boys. They wanted to prove that it was way more fun than having girls. It was a lovely evening filled with laughter, but by the end, the two boys were so wound up that they were bouncing off the furniture, all crazy boy joy. My husband and I were completely overwhelmed. At the very end, our friends looked at us sheepishly and said, "Boys really are great, we promise!"

See? I had every reason to be terrified of having a boy.

As it turns out, we had a few peeing misfires, in the early days (I never bought a Pee Pee Teepee for my own kid), but nothing that hit *me*, thankfully. So far, toilet training my son has been easier than toilet training my daughter. What's been interesting to observe, as my son has grown from infant to toddler to preschooler, is how very different he approaches life than my girls.

I've found myself asking my husband, "Are *all* boys like this?" as I chase after this kid's naked bum, while he tears away from me, screaming and giggling, the moment I take his clothes off to change him. I shake my head as he grabs his penis for the tenth time in ten minutes (my son, not my husband). Our girls never did these things, and are just as baffled by his behavior as I am. My husband just shrugs.

We are not a family who believes that girls wear pink bows and boys wear football jerseys. There's been plenty of mixing things up, in terms of gender roles in our house. My daughter has worn boys' superhero t-shirts, and my son has asked for and happily received barrettes and ponytails in his hair. He has to be like his big sisters, right?

My husband and I are content to let our son explore clothing and adornment in his own way, whether that means tutus or lion costumes. So it's been amazing to see how, without any prompting, this kid *adores* garbage trucks and construction equipment. He also has an encyclopedic knowledge of dinosaurs. The big board book that's filled with trucks, which we've had since my daughter was born, sat on the bookshelf unused for years until my son was born. I tried to read it to my daughter (or rather, read all the different names of different types of service trucks) multiple times, but it could've been a book about the history of cable television, for all she cared. My son, however, has read and looked at it so many times, it is now falling apart at the seams.

And while he loves singing "Let it Go" and pretending to be Anna to his sister's Elsa, if you ask him what he wants to be when he grows up, he'll tell you that he wants to be a dinosaur. And who can blame him? Dinosaurs are pretty awesome. And so are boys, it turns out.

BROTHERLY LOVE

GAIL HOFFER-LOIBL

"When I watch my son play with trucks or chase birds, I am delighted by the boy he is, and during his moments of tenderness, I am delighted by the man he might become." ~Maybe I'll Shower Today

"Please, just go to sleep," I mumbled under my breath as I rocked my toddler, pacing back and forth in my bedroom until I knew every crack on the wall and stain on the carpet. My eyelids resisting the weight of a day spent chasing him and pulling him away from curious hazards extended beyond the point of reasonable sanity. My body aching and sore, longing to collapse on the couch with a piece (ok, maybe more like ten pieces) of chocolate and some Netflix. Has it really been more than an hour of this charade? I was done. I was doner than done. I was the donesiest done that ever doned.

Let me interject here to clarify at his age; I don't have a major issue with putting him down in a crib and letting him cry for a bit. Except there is a bit of a problem.

He climbs out.

If I put him down in a crib, my toddler will American Ninja Warrior his way right out of there, and I am back with a screaming kid and little bit less of my patience.

I am fine with staying with him while he falls asleep. Often, I nurse him peacefully to sleep, enabling me to steal a sliver of calmness from the night air. I gaze upon his tiny eyes, nose, and mouth and still see the fragile newborn I brought into the world nearly two years earlier. His slowed breath and the low rumble of snores let me know I can extract myself from the room. Afterwards, I am able to enjoy an hour or two of peace until both my kids end up in bed with me.

But, even, nursing failed that night.

He screamed, wriggled and pushed on my chest. Wrestling a 20-something-pound child with the strength of a 500-pound gorilla was not how I wanted to spend my evening. Exhausted, I gave up and let go.

I watched from my bed as my son scurried like a cockroach with the lights on down the hall and straight to my oldest son's bedroom.

Do you hear that? The sound of silence.

Parents know quiet often means trouble.

I waited a moment and crept down toward the bedroom. I tiptoed inside, expecting to find my little one knee deep in wipes or pooping on a pile of laundry. Instead, as I peered across the room, I found my toddler sleeping soundly cuddled up next to his older brother.

A warm smile spread across my face, as I let the beautiful moment engulf my body. I marveled at this wonderfully pure display of love unfolding before my eyes.

Then the truth bomb exploded in my brain.

My "baby" literally ran away from me to be with his brother.

Ouch.

I, the one who gave him life, kept him safe and nourished him from my own body, had been replaced.

Were the days of my baby clinging on to me like Velcro coming to an end? Was separation anxiety no longer about me?

My youngest considers his brother the sun, the moon, the stars and the whole massive universe all wrapped up in a four-year-old body. He embodies all the hopes, challenges and dreams a little toddler could want. I love the sounds of pitter pattering feet and giggles as my little one chases his brother around our kitchen. If my oldest is climbing up on top of his bed and leaping on a pile of pillows on the floor below, you can bet my youngest will attempt the same, limited only by his stature and strength. No ladder is too high; no slide is too steep. If big brother can do it, little brother will want to do it too. Even if it means scaring me in the process.

I am the middle child. I know a little something about sibling relationships. I have an older brother and a younger sister. My sister and I were always grouped together. We were the "girls." There were many days when I couldn't stand her and actively tried to get rid of her. She says I once tried to bury her in a pile of stuffed animals (can't confirm). She also likes to remind people I sent her flying out of a shopping cart (that really did happen). I wasn't always a good big sister. I was downright abusive. I'd push her, shove her and even throw her. Yet, she kept coming back. I was her big sister.

I cannot speak for all sisters, and I know the connection between female siblings is special. My sister and I are close, and even though I once wished her back inside my mother's womb, I couldn't imagine my life without her. I understand some sisters speak every day, while others are estranged. I know this is also true for male siblings. But, after observing my kids for nearly two years, I learned the bond between boys is forged with the greatest of strength. Even at their tender ages, I have little doubt these two will do anything for each other. Brothers are the ultimate in the fierce loyalty found in male friendship. This unity is sealed with blood.

My boys' relationship is far from all sweetness and love. For a short while, I foolishly broke up every fight. I would remove my oldest sitting on top of his little brother, only to turn my back and find the baby with his big brother in a sleeper hold. Then, I realized, that's what boys do. They rough house, horseplay, wrestle, or whatever you want to call it. They are in constant contact with one another. Ever see two puppies at play? The pulling, the tugging, and yes, even nipping, are all things I've witnessed with my children. They play hard, and there are many times when they cross the line between fun and dangerous. Because of this, I've adopted the mantra, "Just don't kill each other."

For every push, shove and tackle, there are kisses, hand-holding and head strokes. I cherish the tenderness of my oldest gently encouraging his little brother to walk down the stairs, or of my youngest calling for his big brother the moment his eyes widen in the morning. I hope the devotion and admiration they have for one another will carry them well into adulthood.

For things to flourish, they must be nourished. My boys need their parents to encourage and support them as individuals. We must acknowledge their unique needs and remind them we love them both. While we may have moments of favoring one's behavior over the other, we never want either to feel he is not loved. We, along with the other adults in their lives, will shape their views of the world and one another.

I know boys tend to hold a special place for their mothers. I'm aware of the "mama's boy" jokes and the stories of women bending over backward for their sons. I'm fine with my sons growing to care for one another more than me. I am secure enough to let them go. I will be OK. I may have given them life, but they give each other loyalty, friendship, laughter and incomparable brotherly love.

What I Learned from a Hot Dog

Toni Hammer

"My son's favorite toy is whatever his sister
is playing with." ~Is it Bedtime Yet?

My oldest is a girl which means the second we began telling people that I was pregnant with a little boy we were inundated with well-meaning, but terrifying, advice. I was warned so many times that he would pee on me during diaper changes that I considered buying a poncho. I was told that boys are more dramatic than little girls until they're teenagers and then the drama flips. I was preached to about the best ways to handle boys roughhousing and when to stop allowing him to see me naked and the pros and cons of circumcision and and and... The list went on. In short, everyone's advice always came to the same conclusion: boys are so different from little girls.

They couldn't have been more right about Levi. He does things his own way, in his own time, for his own enjoyment, and doesn't care what anybody else thinks.

The first time he taught me he was very much his own person was when he was around seven months old. With my daughter, we started offering her "real" food around six months. Pureed carrots, bananas, oatmeal, the usual. She gobbled it up like she'd been doing it her whole little life.

Levi, on the other hand, was not having any of it. He wasn't interested in the carrots or peas, showed no interest in bananas, and seemed pretty content to just nurse on demand and maintain the status quo. I knew every kid was different so I didn't push it, didn't worry, and just kept things the same.

Until my husband and I ordered pizza for dinner one night.

My daughter was staying the night with her grandparents, so it was just the three of us. My husband held Levi in his lap while he ate his dinner. Out of nowhere, with the speed and accuracy of a velociraptor, Levi lunged at the pizza in my husband's hand and caught himself a bite to be proud of. Crust, cheese, sauce, toppings and all went into his tiny mouth. Once our shock wore off, we offered him our pizza crust to gnaw on for the rest of the evening.

It was the first time Levi showed me how determined, how different he was. He was going to do things his way in his timing regardless of what everyone else thought.

One day when he was two, we were all in the car on our way to the grocery store. The drive had been quiet until from the backseat I heard a loud voice singing, "LALALALALALAAAAA." Turning around, my darling son has his hands over his ears, was shaking his head rhythmically back and forth, and was serenading himself with some nonsense song. Once I was done laughing, I looked at my husband and told him, "He is special and different in so many ways." My husband agreed. This kid was going to do life his way.

At the time it was cute and adorable and of course made for some good stories, and I loved the fact I had a special little boy, but I didn't know how much his dancing to the beat of his own drum would teach me.

Halloween was three days away and, because their mother is a huge slacker, my kids didn't have costumes. At the first store we visited, my daughter found what she wanted to wear: a costume to transform her into Belle from Beauty and the Beast. Honestly, it could have been any color or design so long as it was a princess dress because she is all dancing and crowns and balls and fairy tales. She was easy to dress for the holiday. Levi was a different story.

Many hours and stores later, after perusing scarce sales rack after sales rack, I was beginning to think we'd just have to cut some eye holes in a sheet and call him a ghost. We went to one final department store as a last ditch effort, and thankfully they still had costumes in his size. The pickings were slim, but they were there. And they were characters he knew! Pikachu, a cowboy and... a hot dog.

Who on Earth would make a kid be a hot dog for Halloween? I thought to myself. Certainly, all kids want to be a person, not something they eat.

Well...

I held up the Pikachu and cowboy costumes in front of him. "Okay, buddy, you pick."

He looked back and forth between the two for what seemed like decades. I was trying to speed things up as I was over shopping and said with an exasperated sigh, "Buddy. Just pick one. Whatever you pick we'll get."

It was then that he bypassed Pikachu, went past the cowboy, and pointed to the hot dog costume with the biggest smile I'd ever seen on his cherubic face.

The foam and felt concoction where his little arms and hands would be in the bun and his head would stick out of the hot dog itself, mustard coating his abdomen. This was what he wanted to be for Halloween. It was his first year choosing his own costume, and he chose this?

"Are you sure, Levi? You don't want to be Pikachu?" I'm embarrassed to admit that I was worried people would think he was weird. That they'd talk about him poorly or make fun of him. I mean, the kid was three and kids that age only care about candy and all the parents would be with all the kids as we trick or treated so, really, I had nothing to worry about in terms of social anxiety but... I'm a mom. A mom who's lived through growing up different and I was fearful of what may happen to him.

He put his foot down though and said he wanted to be the hot dog. I steeled myself, took a deep breath, and gave in. If my son wanted to be a hot dog then a hot dog he would be.

It turned out, as it does with most parenting concerns, I had nothing to worry about. Even better, everybody we passed loved his costume. He was definitely unique – I saw a few girls dressed as Belle like my daughter – but there was only one hot dog. Only one kid who chose to do things his way and embrace who he was and who he wanted to be.

My little boy is special. He is determined and relentless. He doesn't care what other people think about him. He doesn't care how things have always been done. He doesn't care if no one's listening and he wants to sing. He's going to do what he wants to do when he wants to do it.

He recently just turned four, and he's already taught me so much about self-esteem, confidence, and being true to yourself. I know the lessons will continue as he grows and matures and continues to be who he is without fear of anyone's opinions. I can't wait to see what he teaches me next.

Shhhhhhh, Don't Tell Your Brothers, But I Am Enjoying You More

Tove Maren

"When you give a urine sample, do not bring a toddler with you! When he unlocks the door, you WILL miss the cup in an attempt to stop him from opening the door….. or so I am told." ~Mama in the Now

*I*t's past midnight. I crawl under the covers and get in the same position I have slept in for the past three years and four months.

My forehead lightly touches yours. I inhale deeply, taking in the sweet smell of your sleepy exhale. We skipped your bath before bedtime because you fell asleep right after dinner. I close my eyes and the scent of "little boy sweat," and milk-breath fills the air. I immediately drift off into a comfortable slumber.

Throughout the night, you stretch out your arm to constantly have a life-line to me. Your hand finds me; it's your anchor in the darkness. I feel your fingers gently rubbing my arm as you comfortably transition through your sleep stages.

Hours later, the sun is coming through our shutters. Our bedroom is slowly getting brighter, ever so gently, the light is waking us up. I open my eyes to do an inventory of how many kids are in our bed.

There, one inch from my face, are your big brown eyes, staring at me. I don't know how long you have been awake, but without any movement you lay there, watching me sleep. As soon as you see my blue eyes, your face breaks into a big smile, and you shout "Mama! It's mornin' time!"

What three-year-old waits for permission to get out of bed? What three-year-old is perfectly content watching his mother sleep? You, my mama's boy.

You are our fourth son, the one who completed our family. You fulfilled me as a mother.

As soon as your brothers hear that we are awake, they come running, jumping into bed to cuddle and talk about our plans for the weekend.

Last night, before tucking in your older brothers, they asked me if I have a favorite son. Every child asks their parents that question.

I answered truthfully when I said "I love you all equally and differently. I appreciate your individuality, your personalities and all the things you have in common. You get the same amount of love - my whole heart. You have to be a parent to understand how that is possible."

It IS true; I love you all the same. But, shhhhh don't tell your brothers, I am enjoying your childhood more.

When your oldest brother was born, I read every parenting book. Most of them said that he was supposed to be put in his crib while he was still awake. When he woke up, we were supposed to pat his back, and he would quietly drift off again - or at least that's what the book said. Apparently, he never read those books!

He would cry... and cry... and cry some more. I read that we weren't supposed to sleep with him in our bed, the crib was the best place for him, or else he would sleep in our bed until he left for college.

We took turns to hold him, bounce him, rock him, turn on the fan in the bathroom for white noise, and stand next to the running faucet - for more white noise. The poor kid had "white noise overload" - if there is such a thing.

But sleep, he didn't... Until I said "screw it" and brought him into our bed. He's now ten years old and has been out of our bed for 8.5 years - so apparently we didn't mess him up too badly.

Your second brother had medical complications shortly after birth. He spent the first two months in a Pediatric Intensive Care Unit. He never left my arms, once I was finally able to hold him after he got off the respirator. At home, he slept in our bed... he slept... I watched him CLOSELY - his every move, his every breath.

Because of his frail health, we spent the better part of three years living in a big germ-free bubble. The isolation, constant warfare on germs and never-ending worrying wore me down. I spent a lot of time alone with your brother in various doctors' waiting rooms. No child should ever see that many doctors. No parent should worry and search so hard for answers.

I knew that every minute with your brother was a gift and I never once took for granted that he was still with us. However, my brain was in constant overdrive, never able to rest out of fear that I would miss a new symptom.

I read parenting books when your oldest brother was born, and I read medical research reports after your second brother arrived. But nothing I read gave me the answers I was looking for. I kept searching for the holy grail of motherhood advice, oh and we kept having babies too.

Your third brother entered this world more looking like a toddler than a newborn. At 11 lbs. 5 oz., he was a vision of infant health. However, I still read parenting books, worried about germs and heart failure. Everywhere I turned, I saw tell-tale signs of heart disease in your brothers - they were figments of my imagination, thankfully, but it was hard to relax and truly enjoy motherhood.

And then there was you... In one defining moment you showed me that being your mother would be simpler, easier and that I am all you will ever need. Me, the flawed, worried, worn out and tired mother, I gave you life, and I would effortlessly keep you happy - simply because I am MOM.

You were two days old. We were still in the hospital. I had just changed your diaper and dressed you in one of the countless adorable outfits I had packed in my hospital suitcase. The brown and orange outfit complemented your coloring, and it quickly became my favorite outfit for you.

In true newborn-form, you fussed when I dressed you - because who wants to wear clothes when you have been perfectly comfortable in your nakedness for the past nine months.

Your belly was full; I had nursed you before the diaper change. My motherly intuition told me to simply comfort you. I placed you on my shoulder - and that's when the magic moment happened. From that point forward, I knew that mothering you would be different, simpler, stress-free and more enjoyable.

You placed your face in the nape of my neck. I felt your tiny cool nose against my skin. You inhaled deeply, taking in the scent that filled your nose. You let out the sweetest, most satisfied little sigh of contentment - and then you fell asleep right on my shoulder. With every inhale you smelled me again and again - and just knowing that I was near, was enough for you to feel secure, loved and safe enough to sleep.

I let out a silent cry as the tears rolled down my cheeks. You didn't need anything in this world to comfort you, other than the smell of my skin. From that point forward, I knew that our family was complete.

I put away the parenting books, medical journals - even the baby books that I would never complete anyway - and simply enjoyed being the mother of four awesome boys.

The books didn't know my kids, the medical papers never revealed any answers or eased my mind. All along, the only things I should have read were my kids.

Our boys were happier not living "by the books" but rather by "mother's intuition." Since I stopped looking for answers and started following my heart, I became a happier mom.

Shhhhhh… Don't tell your brothers, but YOU showed me how to enjoy motherhood!

I Was Meant To Be a Boy Mom!

Brook Hall

*"My son just told me, "Mama! I peed on
the living room floor, and it looks like a
heart. Come see it." ...You can't make this
stuff up people." ~Stay Home Mama*

I never considered the possibility that I would end up without daughters. I was going to grow up, get married, and have little girls; that is just the way it would be. My future girls and I would play dress up and have tea parties. They would wear darling pink outfits and polka dot bows in their hair. I would paint their nails and let them play with my makeup. I would teach them to shave their legs, take them to buy their first bra, and one day help them pick out a wedding dress. When they were adults, we would be friends who tried on clothes together, shared jewelry and had long chats about life. The idea that I would have boys and only boys never entered my mind. It's just that I never pictured my life any other way. However, in just twelve months and one weeks' time, I went from dreaming of daughters to having two sons. Instead of opening pink dresses and hair bows at my baby shower, I received striped overalls and baby blue blankets. I was heartbroken when I first came to the realization that I may never have a daughter, let alone daughters.

How was I going to handle this? I heard from others that little boys were a ton of fun, but exhausting. I was told that boys were harder to potty train, had lower attention spans, and rarely sat still. I heard horror stories about fearless boys that led me to believe I would have gray hair by thirty. I was scared, overwhelmed, and to be honest, disappointed.

Then came Cooper, my perfect first born. I couldn't have loved him more (not even if he had been a girl) and the joy he brought me erased any disappointment in an instant. In fact, I could not get over referring to him as, "My son" and I said it as often as possible.

When Cooper was just three-months-old, while I was in the thick of it, you know, the sleepless nights, postpartum anxiety, and hair loss, we found out I was pregnant again. (Oops!) A few months later an ultrasound told us that ready or not; we would be adding another boy to the family.

Two boys. Zero girls. Many tears.

Our second son was born via emergency C-section a month early. He had trouble breathing and was transported to a different hospital over an hour away; I couldn't be with him the first two days after he was born. I was only able to see and hold him for a few minutes before he was taken away, but I was already in love and knew that just like his brother, Drake was perfect to me, my handsome little boy.

My boys are now four and five years old. Add in their daddy, and I am outnumbered three to one, but instead of feeling completely left out or like I am missing something, I feel special. I am THE girl in our family, and I am loved in a way that cannot be replicated. My boys and I haven't had any tea parties, but we do love to drink hot chocolate and read stories. We do messy science experiments and play in the dirt. They kill spiders for me with their bare hands and help me carry in the heavy groceries. They pick me flowers and ask me to be their Valentine (even when it is not February). Despite their young ages, they have a strong desire to fight against evil and stand up for what is right; they often dress up as their favorite superheroes, and of course, I always get to be Wonder Woman.

Although there are still times that I long for daughters, something has changed in me. I am aware that if everything I ever wanted would have come to fruition, I wouldn't have these boys; they wouldn't even exist. There is no denying that they can drive me insane and make me want to pull my hair out, but they also get me laughing until tears fall down my cheeks, and they can touch my heart like no one else can. My boys are tough, loud, and stubborn, yet incredibly tender hearted and sweet. These crazy boys who play in the mud, hide toy snakes in my bed, run around the house in capes, masks and never want to wear pants, they are MY boys. I may have never planned on being a boy mom, I may have never believed that it was for me, but I have been proven wrong, and I am happy to admit it. This is my life now, and the joy that comes with it is beyond what I ever could have imagined, these boys are my greatest reward.

I was meant to be a boy mom, and now that I know this, there is nothing else I would rather be--gray hair, muddy floors, exhausting days, and all.

What I Didn't Know

By Dana Kamp

At Swim Lesson...
"Mommy, do you see that wet spot on that tree?"
"Yep, did you pour out your drink?"
"That's my Pee!"
~39ish Life

I didn't know my firstborn would arrive two weeks early, would love to be swaddled, would learn over thirty signs with his little hands, and would make my heart feel like it might burst every time he smiled. And I definitely didn't know the three boys who eventually followed would add more amazement, love, and pure joy to my world than I could have ever imagined.

I had hoped my first child would be a boy -- simply because I really wanted to see my husband with a mini-me. There were so many scenarios I had pictured in my mind. I imagined Jeff teaching him how to play baseball, building sandcastles with him at the beach, and taking him to Gator football games. All of those visions came to fruition ... four times over!

Yes, I have four sons. Yes, we wanted four children. No, I did not keep trying in hopes of getting a girl. I feel like I have that exact conversation with anyone who stops and counts how many little boys are with me. I guess it seems like a lot to many people, but I've grown accustomed to the noise and commotion, the silliness, and infinite energy. I prayed hard for all of that, and it's what makes up my home, my happy place … and I wouldn't change a single thing.

I remember so clearly the day we brought Miles home from the hospital. He was sleeping when we arrived, and I put him gently down in his crib. Jeff and I watched him sleep for a few minutes, then looked at each other and said, "Now what?"

We didn't know what to do next. Should we let him sleep, and go about our day? I was hungry. Should I make a sandwich? Or should we stay near his room so we would hear the first inkling of a cry? He'd be hungry when he woke up, and I needed to be ready to feed him. Our world now revolved around this little human, but we didn't know what that meant.

But, he taught us. He taught us we could meet his needs and ours. I could take a shower, and he'd be just fine in the bouncy seat on the bathroom floor. That yes, it was possible to go to the grocery store and keep him entertained. That kindergarten is hard on mamas, but amazing for the little ones. And most recently, he taught us we didn't have to worry so much about big, bad, scary middle school. While he didn't know what to expect, he wasn't overly anxious about it, and we took his lead.

Miles has been our guinea pig. We were the rookie parents trying out variant methods and philosophies as we went along. From creating our own version of Babywise for him to eventually cosleeping when more babies came along because we were too tired to implement sleep rules. And disciplining with positive reinforcement, then time-out, and then finally realizing each boy would respond differently to each method, so we disciplined them differently, and that worked. While striving to be super parents, we finally learned to just be the parents our boys needed.

It was Miles who taught us all we didn't know about becoming first-time parents. And just a short while into our lessons, we had to teach him how to be a big brother.

I was so excited when we found out our second baby was going to be another boy! A brother for Miles! But, as the due date drew near, I didn't know how I was going to care for two little people, and I didn't know how I was going to give my love fairly to both my 2-year-old and my newborn.

Carson was completely different than Miles. He arrived a day after his due date, he fought every swaddle blanket like it was his job, and he refused to learn more than five signs. But once again, another precious child made my heart swell and added a deep, unimaginable love to my life that I didn't know was possible. I also didn't know that another boy didn't necessarily mean a duplicate. We naively assumed he would be just like Miles. He wasn't and isn't. And I love that.

He taught me I could be a mommy to two unique little boys, loving them equally and fiercely, but also relishing their differences. He taught me that a rough-and-tumble toddler could become a gentle, compassionate tween. That two mischievous boys left unattended will result in some kind of chaos. And that no matter which potty-training method you try, it will suck and there will still be pee on the floor. Life lessons to remember.

Just as we were feeling confident in our multiple-boy parenting, our little wildfire was born. Sawyer's birth was like the lightning speed round of a game show, and his personality was (and still is) that of an eternally happy, no-worries-in-the-world game show host. The boy's goal in life is to smile and make others smile. Whether that happens because of a well-rehearsed knock-knock joke, a hilarious version of a classic nursery rhyme that now includes the words "poop," "puke," or "pee," or a series of frozen facial expressions that get sillier as he goes, he does what it takes to brighten the mood.

I didn't know you could go through this hectic, over-scheduled life without feeling the pressure. I didn't know just stopping and consciously listening to a child's laughter could make you realize that everything is going to be OK.

But, he taught me. Sawyer taught me life is good; no, life is hilarious! Little boys think peeing on trees (or ants) in the backyard is hilarious! Riding a Big Wheel tricycle as fast as possible and then making an incredibly loud skidding drift is hilarious! And even when saying "excuse me" after a burp, it's hard not to laugh because the sound that just erupted from that little face is hilarious! And I have to completely agree.

Two years after our funny boy was born, we were laughing in the ultrasound room as the technician barely touched my belly with the wand, and we immediately saw what we'd seen three times before … a proudly displayed baby penis. Our little caboose was a boy!

Finley has been our family's heart since day one. All three big brothers are enamored with him. At first, I think it was because he was everyone's baby. And then, as he developed his personality, they each began to see a bit of themselves in this little guy. He's a bright, quick learner like Miles, a caretaker like Carson, and a dirt-obsessed outdoors boy like Sawyer. He's the connector that completes our crazy little family.

We knew we wanted four children, but I didn't know labeling a child as your "last one" would bring so much emotion with it. I didn't know seeing our fourth baby become more and more independent would put a knot in my throat. I didn't know that life and especially life with your little ones, really will pass you by if you don't pay attention to it.

But, he taught me. He taught me when a great song comes on, stop what you're doing and dance together. He taught me not to rush hugs. He taught me you could have some of the greatest conversations with a 3-year-old if you sit on the swings with him for a while. And, he taught me it's OK to cry when emotions are bigger than you are.

I didn't know four little boys could be so different.

I didn't know I would love sitting in the sandbox making mud pies and watching lizards.

I didn't know there was a strong mama bear inside of me who would instantly step out of her comfort zone to protect her cubs.

I didn't know I would cry when I thought about not having these loud, silly, wonderful little boys under my roof one day.

I didn't know how to be a boy mom.

But, they taught me. One perfectly lopsided mud pie at a time.

Boys Can Love Nail Polish Too

Britta Eberle

*"When my husband tries to help my son
find something...it's like the blind leading
the blind." ~This is Motherhood*

*M*y four-year-old son has recently discovered his own style. He spikes his hair with gel so that he "looks like a dinosaur." He rarely leaves home without wearing sunglasses - sometimes two pairs at the same time. Occasionally he wears his bike helmet, not because he's going for a ride, just he thinks it's a cool hat. And for some unexplainable reason, he thinks it's fashionable to walk around with his pants pockets turned inside out. He also loves to wear brightly colored nail polish, and his preferred shades are purple and pink.

Wolfy's affection for nail polish started when he was about a year old. One day he was watching me paint my nails, and he stuck out his chubby baby foot. Then he sat perfectly still while I applied it to his impossibly tiny toenails. Through the toddler years, bribing Wolfy with the promise to "do nail polish" was the only way I could get him to sit through clipping his nails. Whatever works, right? Now he is in preschool, and he still loves nail polish. He doesn't think that it's strange or girly and my husband and I have never tried to convince him that it's not appropriate.

Of course, I worry that my son will get teased by other children. He seems like an easy target for bullies when he wears his purple sweatpants and rainbow sneakers to preschool. But I also hope that I am raising a resilient child. And I've hoped that when the day inevitably comes and someone makes fun of him for liking "girl things" that he will shrug it off. I just didn't expect for that day to be today.

While I was in line at the grocery store today, Wolfy ran over to the bench near the register. An elderly woman was already sitting there, but before I could say anything to my son, Wolfy plopped down next to her. As I unloaded my cart and took care of my baby, I also kept one eye on my son sitting on the bench. He smiled at the elderly woman and she smiled back at him. Then they started talking. It was so sweet. I thought to myself, "Talking to my son is probably making this lady's day." They certainly seemed to be getting along.

Then I saw the woman grab my son's hand.

"That's a little strange," I thought, now watching their interaction with my full attention. I strained to hear what they were saying. Over the beeping of the scanner, I thought I caught a word here and there. The woman's voice sounded sharp. And Wolfy didn't look happy anymore.

"Come here, Wolfy!" I called. "What did that lady say to you?" I asked when he was next to me again.

"She told me that I shouldn't have nail polish. She said nail polish isn't for little boys. It's only for girls!"

My heart dropped in my chest. I couldn't believe this was happening. My son was getting harassed in a public place by a stranger.

"What did you say to the lady?"

"I told her that my little sister and I both wear nail polish. And we BOTH like it!"

I squeezed his shoulder. Inside, my heart was pounding. I was so incredibly angry. How dare this woman talk to my son like that? How dare she touch his hand? Does she make it her mission to go around trying to ruin happy childhoods?

I looked up at the bench. It was empty. The mean woman was gone. Wolfy asked if he could go sit down again and I said yes. I started unloading my groceries onto the conveyor belt. And when I looked up, the woman was back! Now I was closer, and I could hear her say, "Now that I've told you that nail polish is only for girls, are you going to go home and take that stuff off?"

I couldn't believe it. She was still bothering my kid! I was stuck. Do I go over there and leave my baby in the cart? Do I yell for Wolfy to come back to me? What should I say to her? I didn't want to cause a scene. But before I could make a decision, I heard Wolfy's answer.

"No," he said, "I'm not going to do that. I like nail polish, and so does my little sister!"

My son doesn't wear nail polish to make a statement. He doesn't wear nail polish to bend gender roles and challenge stereotypes. He simply wears it because he thinks it looks neat. That's it. My son's days of not having this awareness are numbered. And this woman tried to make them even fewer. She tried to take away his innocence. It wasn't her place. It was rude, and it was downright mean.

At first, I felt sorry for my son. I worried that he might feel embarrassed and ashamed. But as I thought about it more, I realized that it's not him that I should pity. It's her. She's the person who lives in a sad, narrow world. It's a world without self-expression. It's a world without choices. And her world is so weak and so fragile that the unintentional choices of a four-year-old boy threaten to destroy it.

I doubt that the interaction with my little boy changed the woman's life in any way. I'm pretty sure that she left the grocery store shaking her head. What a little freak. A misfit. A weirdo. And the truth is that Wolfy is none of these things. My son is just an intelligent, strong-willed child with big brown eyes. But you know what? If he turns out to be a weirdo or a freak, I'm okay with that too. The thing that changed that day in the grocery store was the way that I saw my son. I realized that he's stronger and more confident than I ever imagined and I will never underestimate him again.

Expecting the Unexpected

Alison Tedford

"Daily odd compliment from my son: "If
Superman had a mom like you, his underwear
would be on correctly under his pants not
on top!" ~Sparkly Shoes & Sweat drops

I didn't expect to have a boy. I figured I would have a girl. After all, I knew what to do with girls. I was raised as the eldest of four girls, and while I wasn't a girly-girl, I knew how to play with girls and how to take care of them. As far as dealing with boys, I was clueless.

Fast forward to the day I pushed that cute, squishy kid into the waiting hands of a doctor and they announced, "It's a boy!" You could have knocked me over with a feather, and not just because I was exhausted from four hours of hard work. FOUR, I know. You probably hate me right now reading that, and I'm truly sorry. But enough about you, we were talking about me.

I didn't know what to do with a boy. I was surprised, a little nervous (a LOT nervous) and also overwhelmed with impostor syndrome. All of these people seemed to think I should know what I'm doing and be okay. I was twenty-five, after all. I didn't know what to do, truthfully. He seems to be fine, so I guess I underestimated myself. I didn't know what I was getting myself into, but I figured it would eventually be pretty smelly. I wasn't wrong.

Thus began my adventure as a boy mom. I learned that you could make any everyday object into a truck if you just make the appropriate noises as you move it back and forth on the floor (even a tissue box will do!) I learned that a potty making truck noises is not enough incentive to use it, but is still wildly entertaining. Boymomhood has been a learning experience. Even though I was expecting a girl and was a little disoriented, I wasn't disappointed in having a boy.

To be honest, I was a little relieved that I had a boy, as I knew all too well how easily I could have become ensnared and bankrupted by the aisles of lacy dresses and pretty girly shoes. As a boy mom, my main criteria for selecting my son's clothes were: 1) Does it smell (badly?) 2) Is it ripped (noticeably?) 3) Does it fit (approximately?) That being said, for special occasions when he was a baby, I would dress him up like a little banker in snazzy sweater vests, which might have had something to do with the delicate spirit he became.

He was soft like those little sweater vests. My little boy wasn't a rough and tumble boy. He was sensitive and sweet, desperately concerned with the water quality in Africa and the prevalence of heart disease. He hated getting dirty and wasn't into sports until one day he announced his intentions to play lacrosse. Boy, were we surprised!

Seemingly overnight my not-so rough and tumble boy became a mass of sweat wielding a big stick with skinned knees that he barely noticed. The softness of his sweater vests had ridden up to reveal a warrior, a champion and the proud owner of a new jock strap. I have never felt as awkward as I did the day we bought that. It was another reminder of the unexpected blessing I didn't quite know what to do with but muddled through awkwardly with joy.

He wasn't what I expected, but it turns out he was even more than I could have hoped for. In the end, he helped me become more than I could have ever imagined. I think our mirrored awkwardness and uncertainty brought us closer because we were just two people navigating our way through a new adventure (one of us in a snazzy sweater vest.)

THE BIG BROTHER

JENNIFER WEEDON PALAZZO

"Some nights, I tell my son it's bedtime an hour and a half before...he can't tell time." ~Mom Cave TV

I'm not a spiritual, New-Age, premonition-having type person. But for some inexplicable reason, I always knew my first child would be a boy. When I became pregnant the first time, at an ultrasound I'll never forget, we found out that the child I was carrying would not make it. As we were digesting this terrifying, life-changing information, we didn't even consider asking the baby's sex. The stone-faced technician told us, "And by the way, it's a boy."

Over the next few years, in our journey towards having a family, I still had a very strong feeling that I'd have multiple children and the oldest would be a boy. But was my feeling based on a live boy here on earth or the one we had already lost?

When I became pregnant the second time, we were waiting on tenterhooks for each milestone test result. I was afraid to get too attached in case this pregnancy also had problems. We breathed a little sigh of relief with each normal test result. And this time I wanted ALL the information, as quickly as possible. So as soon as the sex could be determined, we heard those words again, "It's a boy."

With that pronouncement, somehow I felt like things would be all right. And they were. He is now almost seven years old, and the picture of good health. He climbs trees, collects rocks, catches bugs, and whittles twigs into spears. All the Norman-Rockwell-esque boyishness I had foreseen.

But he also takes tap dancing classes (with me!), loves clothes shopping (he is his mama's son!) and baking, knits, and pretends to "nurse" his baby sister.

Yes, he has a baby sister. With that pregnancy, we decided to keep the sex a surprise. My intuition was wrong that time--I felt like I was having yet another boy. I'd been a "boy mom" for five years by then. I felt like I had a handle on boys. I've rarely seen my husband so weepy and sheepish as the moment when the doctor let him "call it" in the delivery room. "We have a girl," he announced to the birthing team. And with that pronouncement, I wondered if my "premonition" about having a boy first had anything to do with the fact that I, the eldest of my siblings, had longed for an older brother. The relationship between big brother and little sister has always been one I've envied.

So the boy I once imagined, dreamed of, and longed for, has manifested into a fully complex and fascinating individual, and a protective and attentive big brother. The little girl I never knew I wanted is the light of our lives. I can't wait to see how the big brother, little sister dynamic unfolds as they grow.

MY GENTLE GIANT

SUSANNE KERNS

*"Boys: Sweet little humans who can be
cuddling a teddy bear one second and
tying it to an art easel for Nerf-gun target
practice the next." ~SusanneKerns.com*

*I*n psychology, The Duality of Man refers to the two opposing sides of human nature. Good versus evil, emotional versus rational, or sweet and gentle versus a loud, crashing, destructive menace.

Which brings me to my seven-year-old son, who my husband and I affectionately refer to as, "The Gentle Giant."

The 'giant' part is because, at over four and a half feet tall, he is off-the-charts on the pediatrician's growth chart, towering over most other first graders, (and even some fifth graders.)

The gentle is because he frequently does things like stop bike traffic on the way to school to let a roly poly safely cross the sidewalk. His tender heart requires fair and kind treatment of everyone, which explains why we once had to stop reading "James and the Giant Peach" after the wicked aunts called James a few bad names. Even this fictional cruelty resulted in inconsolable tears as he asked, "Why would they say that to James? People shouldn't be mean to each other!"

Despite all his sweetness and his gentle heart, living with this loving boy for the past seven years has given me a new understanding about the duality of man: Even the gentlest of giants are hardwired to destroy.

Now, I don't mean *destroy* in a malicious or sociopathic, "light my sister's dolls on fire" way. He's more like a curious giant who accidentally crushes an entire village because he's not paying attention while chasing a butterfly. Or an excited Labrador whose wagging tail takes out everyone's wine glasses on the coffee table while he simultaneously tears the head off of his chew toy simply because he wants to see what's inside of it.

Fortunately, his dueling sides have managed to live together in yin and yang harmony, bringing balance to the mayhem in our home.

When he was a toddler, the gentle part of him quietly played for hours in his Little Tykes kitchen, taking dozens of lunch orders and preparing plates filled with plastic hotdogs and eggs while dressed in an ensemble complete with apron, chef hat, and oven mitt. However, at the same time, his inner giant was busy researching which Melissa and Doug wooden fruits could most easily be confused for balls. Then, if I gave my "we only throw balls in the house," lecture, he could feign innocence about mistaking the heavy, wooden orange for a ball while still maximizing his throwing distance thanks to its extra mass.

As he got older, our gentle giant moved into his construction phase. His gentle side played non-stop with wooden blocks, building elaborate, gravity defying buildings to house and protect his vast collection of Bob the Builder trucks and animal figurines. But, eventually his giant side could no longer take all the cuteness, so he would bulldoze through his block town, the sounds of crashing blocks accompanied by his dramatic screams on behalf of the dinosaurs and the cast of Bob the Builder being crushed beneath the rubble.

And now there are the Legos. Oh, the Legos. Nothing brings more peace and quiet (and clutter) into our home than a new Lego set. His little engineer brain thrives on the order and methodical nature of constructing Legos. This originally led me to believe that he inherited my Type A, Lord Business side, but it didn't take long to discover that he's a Master Builder, or technically a Master Destroyer. He'll meticulously follow the instructions to assemble a 1,329 piece Millennium Falcon for the express purpose of destroying it the second the last piece is snapped into place. What I see as a hard-earned, completed masterpiece, he sees as a mass of Lego potential energy, straining to break free. Whereas I see the destroyed pile as a 'waste' of fourteen hours of work, he sees it as an opportunity to recreate.

Even virtual worlds are not safe from my gentle giant. When he first started playing Minecraft, he would create worlds for me, building massive brick structures that spelled out "Mom" and asking all my favorite colors and animals so he could build a little mommy utopia. He would collaborate with his best friend, sharing diamonds, iron, and emeralds in the civilized and democratic pixelated world they created together. What a wonderful game, I thought! That's until the fateful day I peeked over his shoulder and asked "whatcha building, sweetie?" He replied, "I built this big wall and then dug to the end of the world inside it and then spawned a bunch of sheep in there, so they have to jump into the end of the world!"

What was that I said earlier about not being a sociopath?

But just when I think it's time to call in a professional to address my son's virtual animal torture, I catch him in this room, quietly tucking his stuffed animals into a bed he prepared on his floor so the little plush friends that couldn't fit in his bed wouldn't feel left out.

Or hugging his stuffed bear, Teddy, with tears in his eyes when they were playing Sorry! together and he had to take out one of Teddy's pieces.

Or using his free time in school to make his sister a 'Get Well' card after she broke her foot.

Or the dozens of other heartfelt, loving gestures he makes every day to his family, friends, pets and any (non-Minecraft) creature that crosses his path.

I know that I only have a few precious years left until puberty and hormones start to chip away at the gentleness of my giant. Soon, he'll be fluent in a medley of bad words that would make the evil Aunts in James and the Giant Peach blush. But no matter how old or big my giant becomes, I will always be reminded of the gentle, little boy who could not go to sleep until his collection of nine special stuffed animals was accounted for.

And I think I'll keep Teddy around, just in case my son ever needs some reminding too.

AN ORANGE BUTTERFLY DAY

ERIN CURLETT

*"I never thought I'd be offering my son a tampon
at bath time each night, saying "okay, here's
your squid!" But he's made up a theme song and
a bath dance, and he's learning about science,
so you know, trade offs."~Truthfully Told*

*H*is tiny arms and legs fly at me the moment I walk through the classroom door.

"Mommy! Hold me!"

My two-year-old's face tells me a story of fear. Jacob never asks to be held—unless he is stalling at bedtime—so I lower myself gingerly to his level, trying not to tip myself over from the weight of his baby brother in the Bjorn on my chest.

Jacob buries his face into my hair, his tan arms encircling my neck. His teacher walks over quickly, her concern acute, as I struggle to stand under the weight of my boys.

"He had a really good day," she begins. "But that was because he spent most of it inside. Has he ever been stung by a wasp? He was terrified today."

The answer to her question is no, though I can't understand why it would take being stung by a wasp to experience terror at the thought of them, much less in the face of one.

"We saw a wasp the other day," I reply. "I probably made it into a bigger deal than I should have."

It had been a big wasp, all legs and wings and buzzing near my ear before I slammed the car door shut on it and the heat of the day. I squealed, and Jacob had asked why. "It was a wasp! Those things are scary; I'm glad it didn't get me!"

And thus his terror of wasps began.

Then we started reading *Anamalia*, that gorgeous picture book of alphabet and animals that always fascinated me as a child. Toward the end of the book is a page on which warrior wasps seem to fly out toward the reader, fearsome weapons clutched with their spindly legs. Jacob had spent too much time staring at the unseemly insects, asking me question after question about what wasps do, where they live, how bad is their sting.

When I was a girl, I think I skipped that page.

At the beginning of that same book is a sticker with a black cat and the words "Ex Libris," and under that, in smaller letters, "Timmy." The book belonged to my husband as a child, and since my husband had deployed to Afghanistan, Jacob and I had been reading it often to feel close to him.

The day Jacob runs from the wasps, Tim has been away for five months. We have no certainty of when he will return.

"It was a wasp day, Mommy," Jacob whispers into my neck. "It was a wasp and bee day. They have stingers, and they want to sting me."

When I learned our first child was going to be a boy, I allowed myself twenty-four hours to grieve. I had convinced myself the baby I carried was a sweet, emotional little girl, my miniature, someone I could talk to and relate to. *What am I going to do with a little boy? I know nothing.* The tears fell unbidden as Tim, and I watched the sonogram screen, our son's maleness so clear against the darkness.

"I won't be able to talk to him," I said to Tim over greasy burgers later that day. "He won't share with me how he's feeling. What am I going to do? How will we have a relationship?"

My assumption was that if we had a little boy, he would be a carbon copy of his dad: light-hearted, quick to laugh, treading carefully when emotions are at·play.

What I didn't realize then was the boy curled in the quiet of my womb was a miniature version of his mama: intense, sensitive, with big emotions he'd wear recklessly. I didn't know that at eighteen-months-old he'd be sobbing in my arms after watching "Five Little Ducks" on the iPad because his sadness at the separation of Mother Duck from her ducklings was too much to bear.

It is bedtime, and Jacob is mad. He refuses to lie down for his diaper change, kicking and hitting me as I make the attempt. His violent refusals are wearing on my patience. I know there was something simmering beneath his behavior, but I don't have the energy to try and unearth it. Not tonight. Both boys have been waking in the night, and I am exhausted.

His diaper changed, I put him in his crib and turn out the light. He is yelling, and when I pick him up to sing him his special song, he smacks me with his hand. And that's it. I snap. Every mom yells, but this is more. This is anger; this is mean. I see it in the way his deep brown eyes widen, his face crumpling as he pushes himself into the corner of his crib—as far away from me as he can get.

"No, Mommy!" He sobs, but he doesn't look sad. He is terrified.

I crumple, too.

"Oh, no, Buddy." I lower my voice. "What's wrong? Are you scared?"

"Yes," he continues to sob.

"Are you scared . . . of me?"

He looks up into my eyes, eyes that look so much like his own. His breath hitches. "Yes, Mommy."

In that moment, the world shifts. My child—my precious boy, for whom I'd do anything to protect—is afraid of me. Like wasps, like bees, like the deadly centipedes who circle our house, I have given him something to fear.

How quickly my anger seeped into this room, how quickly I changed. I understand why he is afraid.

I've been there, too: I watched as my dad—my loving, protective, heart-of-gold dad—give into the anger and become unrecognizable, if only for a moment.

There is a difference between stern and mean, between words that stop and words that sting.

"Seems like maybe Mommy needs to take a couple of deep breaths," I say quietly. He watches closely as I inhale deeply, exhaling as slowly as I can.

He needs to see me catching myself, paying attention to the big emotion, naming it, and letting it go. He has to know this process isn't easy, that messiness is inevitable.

He lets me pick him up, and as I cradle him in my arms, he rests his head on my shoulder.

The truth is I am afraid someday Tim won't return home to me. I am afraid I'll lose the love of my life, my partner, my friend. But mostly, I am afraid my boys will lose their dad.

The fear threatens to consume me, to turn to poison in my veins. And when I am cornered, that poison turns into a venomous sting.

But that's not who I want to be.

Care-free and kind. Gentle. Slow to anger. These are qualities that drew me to Tim, and in our time together his influence has softened me. When he is away, I tend to forget.

I have my moments: we have dance parties in the kitchen, and Jacob laughs so hard he giggles himself into hiccups. We turn the hose on high and splash in the mud, jump in the kiddie pool fully clothed. We have tickle fights and roll down the grassy hill in the yard.

We laugh away the loneliness, the boys and I. We have to. When you're mothering boys, letting go becomes an essential daily practice.

But I need my husband to remind me it doesn't always have to be so hard. I need to watch him soaring on the wind, seeking nothing but the beauty of the moment, the sweetness of flight.

When I go to pick up Jacob from school, his teacher smiles at me. "He had another great day."

Since the baby is home with Tim, my arms are free to scoop up Jacob and hold him close.

"How was your day, Buddy?"

He smiles. "Today was not a wasp day. Today was an orange butterfly day."

Of course it was. His dad is home now. Our house could lift off the ground; the air is so light. Laughter fills our hallways. We dance like the orange butterflies Jacob chases in our yard.

Jacob continues, "There was a kind wasp, Mommy. It didn't sting me."

As I carry him to the car, my first baby, the one who made me a mother, I'm struck by the glorious weight of him.

Let me learn to be a butterfly, too, I think. *Let me show him how to soar.*

Skinny Dipping

*"I am not very perfect at parenting, but I
do love my sons enough to cuddle with them
while they smell like pee, and I feel like
that's kind of a lot." ~Wonderoak Blog*

I have one son that I do not understand at all.
He is like part caveman or something.

100% of the time he is coated with dirt and has dried leaves
and sticks poking out of his curly hair. When I send him in for a shower,
he comes out looking exactly the same.

Me: "Did you wash your hair?"

Him: "WHAAAAAT???" (Total shock like he's never bathed before). "You never told me to do that."

Me: "Did you wash your...never mind...get back in there and wash
ALL THE THINGS."

"Butt and pits!" I holler after him because if there's one thing I've
learned from raising this boy, it's that subtleties ARE lost on him.

He's the one who leaves all the sinks in the house running, who cuts
the carpet with a pocket knife to hide his "treasures" inside, and who
forgets to bring his shoes to the grocery store.

Cave-son is also a hoarder. He has been buying and finding junk
since he could walk. He's always found discarded toys, balls, and plastic
rhinestones where ever we go. He gets this from his Grandpa whose
office is lined with trinkets and guitars he got off of eBay. My life goal

is to keep eBay a secret from cave-son forever. He has a particular love for fake gold watches and statues with crystal dolphins on them, and he is currently begging us to let him save up for either a tobacco pipe (like Grandpa's) or throwing knives.

God help us all.

My other son is the king of responsibility. He is cautious, calculated, and hates getting in trouble. If you asked him a question about the NFL or Kane Toads, you better be prepared to turn old and gray before he is done telling you the facts.

He is ten now, and he is like a giant who is never aware of his body. He runs into me constantly. Also, he just developed B.O. so I can smell him coming to trip over me with his massive feet. He is more self-aware than cave-son, but not enough to notice that his hair looks like he recently got electrocuted 95% of the time.

His main character flaw is that he is a morning person. He asks me for a play-by-play of the day's plans before I've had my coffee. My mouth doesn't even work properly at that time so I usually just say "no."

Him: "So! What are we doing today?!"

Me: "No."

Him: "What are we having for breakfast?"

Me: "No."

He is Will Farrell from Elf, and I'm the grumpy dad who doesn't want syrup and noodles for breakfast.

He looks at me like a hyper quivering puppy ready to pounce with more questions.

Me: "NO."

My boys couldn't be more different, but both of them are skilled in the art of nose-picking, sister-torturing, and hell-raising.

I used to consider myself fun before I had kids. I was always up for an adventure or a party. I loved (still love) to have a good time, but these boys have seriously put me to the test. Sometimes mothering feels more like being a full-time lifeguard, risk assessor, and fun-quencher.

The cautious son always asks for permission first (thank God). Things like, "Mom, can my cousins and I drive your car around the pasture?"

YOU ARE TEN, WHAT ARE YOU EVEN SAYING TO ME?

The cave-son never asks. I just find him digging in the sand box with my steak knives.

We took a trip recently, and one night I took the kids to swim at the beach with my friend. It was nearing sunset, and the beach was fairly quiet. The boys jumped in the water immediately and were attacking each other like crazed lunatics. I was calling out the usual mom-isms like, "stop punching!" and "please don't jump on each other's heads!"

My cave-son called out with bright eyes, "Hey Mom, can we skinny dip?"

Apparently my husband had enlightened them about nude swimming.

"Sure," I said.

They stared at me in stone-cold silence until suddenly cave-son's eyes popped out of his head and he started screaming in ecstasy. Cautious-son continued to stare blankly.

"All you need to do is slip off your shorts and hold them in your hand while you swim," I said.

In a matter of seconds, cave-son held his red trunks above his head and hollered like George of the Jungle.

"Doesn't it feel glorious?" I asked.

Cautious-son continued to look at me like, "who are you and what have you done with my mother?" but slowly a sly smile crept across his face.

Cave-son started whooping like a rodeo cowboy swinging his shorts over his head like a lasso. Soon, I saw cautious-son's hand creep to the surface. Out came white shorts. Slowly, he raised them above his head in calculated triumph, with a grin on his face so wide I thought it might crack in half.

They laughed and swam like chimpanzees that had been released from the zoo.

Wild laughter echoed across the water; they were entirely in their element.

They were about forty-feet out when a couple of girls around their age started walking by us on the beach. The boys' bodies were hidden in the dimming light, but I watched their eyes widen. Cave-son let out a "WOOOP!" and swung his shorts above his head proudly.

I'm glad to see he already knows how to impress a girl at the ripe age of eight.

Cautious son giggled uncontrollably until they walked out of sight.

I am often the over-protector of the family, shutting down sketchily hatched plans that will lead to certain ER visits. These boys, they march to their own tunes. Or maybe its coyote howls? I'm not sure. It's a sound that calls them into the deep unknown and begs them to devour life at its fullest. They may do it differently, but they both do it.

They are covered in dirt and sap, and their fingernails are permanently stained black. They pick their noses and would wear the same pair of shorts FOREVER if I let them. I sometimes understand 10% of what they are talking about.

As their mom, I desire to make sure they keep growing and thriving and that they don't brand each other with the iron marshmallow roasters. It's my job to sit them down and tell them, FOR THE RECORD I DO NOT WANT TALK OF DRIVING MY CAR FOR SIX MORE YEARS AT LEAST, CAPICHE? I want to teach them to be kind, and safe, and intentional in the way they lead their lives.

I also want to let them answer the call of the wild whenever I can.

That night it was skinny dipping.

My favorite thing is at the end of the day; my boys cuddle close. They ask me to scratch their backs, and they lay their heads on my shoulders. At that point, I don't care if we have to talk about Kane Toads and throwing knives. I don't care if they're a little stinky or sticky. I love my boys. Cave-son squeezes my arm and says, "I love you mom." Cautious-son snuggles in close.

I love when I get a chance to say yes to their wild. Yes, you can build a fire in the fire-pit. Yes, you can carve that piece of drift wood.

Yes, you can swim naked.

Live it up boys.

MINE!

LYNDEE BROWN

*"A boy's motto: Snacks are life and clothing
is always optional."~#Lifewithboys*

Birth:

I stare in awe at you.

You open your slate blue eyes at me and stare back.

We are suspended in a moment in time.

Everyone else fades away, and I feel this overwhelming
need to cry with joy.

I want to shout, "Mine!"

Everyone should know you gave me this happiness.

All I can do is gasp. I am utterly speechless.

My heart is so full it could burst at any moment.

I know at that moment, our moment, I would do anything for you.

I would protect you with my life always.

I now realize you are more important than myself.

You are my son. I am your mother.

Welcome to our world. I will make sure your possibilities are endless.

Beyond:

I stare in awe at you.

Your hazel brown eyes look down at me.

We are suspended in a moment in time.

Everyone else fades away.

I still want to shout, "Mine!"

I hand you over to dance with the woman you love.

The one who came after me.

The one who you will spend your life with.

You will always protect her.

I will always protect you, fiercely.

You are my son. I am your mother.

ABOUT THE AUTHORS

Jennifer Bairos lives in Toronto, Ontario, Canada with her husband, her son, and their surprisingly vicious cat. When she's not blogging, Jenn teaches middle school, and she is an avid reader. She has also somehow been roped into completing Tough Mudder Half events each summer with her colleagues. Jenn's writing has been featured on Mental Health on The Mighty, Yummy Mummy Club, and the TODAY Parents Funniest Facebook roundup. Find more from her on her blog www.asplendidmessylife.com as well as on Facebook @asplendidmessylife and her bookish Instagram account @jennbairos.

Katia Bishops is the creator of IAMTHEMILK, a Wordpress recommended blog in the family category (2014-2015). Katia spent thirty years wanting to write and making excuses for not doing it. It took immigration and a challenging second pregnancy to start (don't try this at home). Since she started blogging in 2012 Katia was part of RedBook Magazine's blogger team, Netflix's StreamTeam and her writing was featured on multiple websites and in print. Katia is a mother of two who must have done something really bad in her previous life which she is paying for now by not sleeping. She channels her frustration via memes on her Facebook page and her creativity via Instagram.

Rachael Boley is a single mom to her three boys: identical twin five-year-olds and a four-year-old. She works full time as an addictions therapist and spends her "spare time" being a soccer mom. Coffee is her soulmate, her boys are her heroes, and she has learned everything beautiful in this life by just continuing to show up in the middle of every crazy, messy thing. Her brokenness has become her redemption and motherhood has given her the world.

Lyndee Brown is Haden and Ryland's mom. She has been married to her husband Matt for ten years. She has a bachelor's of science degree and works as a Respiratory Therapist during the day. At night she moonlights as Superwoman. She is very fluent in sarcasm and can burn toast with the best of them. She is the co-founder of the blog hashtagl-lifewithboys.com.

Amber Christensen is the mother of four ball-kicking, grilled-cheese eating, tower-building boys who prides herself on being a boy bathroom cleaning survivor. Amber is the author of Memoirs of Mayhem: The Good, The Bad, and The Hilarious. Available on Amazon, it illustrates how even mundane tasks like carpool and laundry can be humorous!

Erin Curlett lives with her husband and two boys on the windward side of Oahu. When she's not in the middle of a toddler dance party or tickle fight, Erin loves to jog by the ocean, play with eye makeup, and send super long voice messages to her friends. Erin writes because she believes vulnerably sharing our stories with each other is the best way to heal, connect, and find hope in the future. Former blog editor of the Good Mother Project, Erin's writing has also appeared on Mamalode, Scary Mommy, and her personal blog, www.erincurlett.com

Britta Eberle lives in rural Vermont with her husband and two children. She loves gardening and pickling the things that she grows. She's a Youth Services Librarian and writes about parenting on her site; This Is Motherhood.

Ashford Evans lives with her husband, three children, and three dogs in South Carolina. When she's not pregnant, breastfeeding, or polishing off a bottle of wine she is busy holding down her sales career or working at their family owned business. She blogs about her crazy escapades and living life in between being the bread winner and the bread maker at biscuitsandcrazy.net. Most recently she became known as "the urinal cake lady" (for real ya'll google it). She has been featured in US Weekly, Independent Review Journal, Pop Sugar, Mom Babble, Scary Mommy, and the Huffington Post.

Suzanne Fleet is the New York Times Best-selling author and humorist behind the award-winning blog, Toulouse & Tonic. A contributor to the Huffington Post and Today.com, Suzanne is perhaps best known for spending too much time in her pajamas. This story marks Suzanne's 6th anthology appearance. She's currently working on a funny book about sick kids. The only way to figure that one out is to put it on your future reading list. Mom to two stinky boys and wife to a very self-assured man, Suzanne makes fun of them, herself and everyone else in print and on all social media @toulousentonic.

Sabrina Greer is a wife and mom to three boys: Oliver (11), Sterling (2.5) and Walker (6 months). She is a Lifestyle Entrepreneur managing multiple home-based businesses and a writer/blogger. Her book on smashing through self-limiting beliefs launched in June and her mommy blog can be followed at www.momofboys.me. Sabrina's pre-motherhood journey was that of a fast-paced, globe-trotting, fashion model, food and beverage consultant giving her rich experiences and a positive outlook on life and parenting alike.

Brook Hall has always wanted to make people laugh, lucky for her she gave birth to two hilarious boys who give her more than enough material to work with. She spends all her time at home taking care of her two little comedians, while also trying to squeeze in moments alone with her hubby. Brook can be found on her blog Stay Home Mama. Her favorite times of day are nap time, bed time and when she gets a new "like" on Facebook.

Toni Hammer is an author, freelance writer, professional joke teller, and stay-at-home mom. She doesn't like anything pumpkin spiced and doesn't know what she'll do with her life once both her children are in school. Please send ideas.

Karsson Hevia is a mother to two little dudes working as a content writer, blogger and social media strategist in the Bay Area (while maintaining her deep Midwest roots). Karsson writes about the excruciatingly beautiful juxtaposition of motherhood and her continual desire to find the so-called balance of life on her blog: 2manyopentabs.

Gail Hoffer-Loibl is the mother of two beautiful, spirited boys, who have taught her endless lessons on life, love and never being able to get rid of the smell of pee in your bathroom. She writes about the joys, trials and funny parts of parenting, motherhood, and raising young men on her blog, Maybe I'll Shower Today. Her work has been featured on The Huffington Post, Her View from Home, Sammiches and Psych Meds, Scary Mommy, The Good Men Project and more. She received her Bachelor's Degree in English Literature and Rhetoric from the State University of New York at Binghamton.

Bianca Jamotte LeRoux is a mom, actress, award-winning filmmaker, Brooklyn business owner, and creator of the original independent series *Real Mommy Confessions*. Her acting career began in musical theater and quickly turned to commercials, print, and recurring roles in soap operas *One Life to Live* and *As the World Turns*. Her notable stage appearances include starring as Fantine in *Les Miserables* and Velma Von Tussle in *Hairspray*. Bianca's most exciting role to date is undoubtedly her job as mom, which brings on a daily host of challenges and accomplishments, often simultaneously. These include successfully keeping her four-year son old from nose diving off the sofa, as well as negotiating with her willful five-year old daughter. Bianca is looking forward to continuing combining her experiences in the film industry and those as a mother into one with the newest season of *Real Mommy Confessions*, scheduled to shoot in spring 2018.

Karen Johnson is a former English teacher who writes at The 21st Century SAHM. She is also an assistant editor for Sammiches and Psych Meds and a regular writer for Babble, Her View from Home, and KC Parent Magazine. Karen and her family live in the Kansas City area in a house that's never clean but is full of joy and laughter. And her wine fridge is always full. You can follow Karen on Facebook, Twitter, and Instagram as The 21st Century SAHM.

Jessica Johnston is mom to four kids. She specializes in coffee drinking and TMI sharing. She is the writer behind wonderoak.com, and her work has been featured on the Huffington Post, Scary Mommy, ABC News, Today Parents, and Motherly.

Dana Kamp is the founder and content creator at 39ishlife.com, as well as a freelance writer and editor. She lives in Florida with her husband and four boys, where they go outside every day to burn energy, get dirty, and pee on trees (the boys, not Dana).

Susanne Kerns is a Writer and Marketing Consultant living in Austin, TX with her husband and two children. Her stories have been featured in the books, "But Did You Die?" "I Just Want to Be Perfect," "It's Really 10 Months - Special Delivery," and "Martinis & Motherhood: Tales of Wonder, Woe & WTF?!" as well as a variety of websites, including her blogs, SusanneKerns.com and The Dusty Parachute. Susanne is also the Co-Producer of the Listen to Your Mother show in Austin. Follow her on Facebook to see why she's frequently featured on Today Parents' "Funniest Parents on Facebook" round-up. She's also on Instagram, where she posts her tasteful nudes.* (*Mostly photos of poorly lit food, and animals, all nude.) You can also find her on Twitter whenever she accidentally opens the wrong app on her phone.

Tove Maren is a Danish/ American mother of four boys. She reports live from the trenches of motherhood on her blog "Mama in the Now". Through her writing, she is helps other mothers to parent with heart and humor, and not take life TOO seriously.

Jennifer Martin is a Canadian mom to three handsome boys aged eight, nine, and eleven as well as a very feisty Australian Shepherd puppy. After having three boys in three years, she was inspired to create a boy mom community to celebrate the joys and trials of raising the opposite gender. When she's not at her desk working on her blog Mom vs. the Boys, you can usually find her in the kitchen baking, behind the camera, or exploring the great outdoors with her family.

Leslie Means is the co-founder and owner of Her View from Home. She is also a former news anchor, published children's book author, weekly columnist, and has several published short stories as well. She is married to a very patient man. Together they have two fantastic little girls ages nine and seven and one little dude born in March of 2017. When she's not sharing too much personal information online and in the newspaper, you'll find Leslie somewhere in Nebraska hanging out with family and friends. There's also a 75% chance at any given time, you'll spot her in the aisles at Target.

Lisa Munn, the Sarcastic Mommy, is currently trying to be queen of her all-male household. She resides in California with her husband and four sons. You can find her sharing her sarcastic parenting humor on Twitter, Facebook, and Instagram.

Tiffany O'Connor is a mom to two amazing, energetic, and fearless human boys and one loveable furry boy dog. She is married to her high school sweet heart and has three college degrees. She is a successful freelance writer, managing editor of Papillion Parent, and has been published in Chicken Soup for the Soul. Her hobbies include watching TV shows about zombies, hiding in her hot tub with a glass of champagne, listening to Taylor Swift songs on repeat, and writing all about her misadventures parenting in a "man cave." She chronicles her experiences raising boys at hashtaglifewithboys.com.

Mikenzie Oldham is a #boymom. She lives on a farm with her husband, twin boys and any number of new animal friends. She is a hope dealer, social media designer, finder of four shoes and super hero side-kick. You can follow all their shenanigans on FB #meandallmyboys.

Glynis Ratcliffe used to be an opera singer, but after her daughter begged her to stop singing and be quiet for the millionth time, she decided to use her inside voice and write instead. Now, she's a freelance writer with bylines at The Washington Post, Scary Mommy, Romper, and CBC, as well as being a copywriter and ghostwriter for anchor clients in various industries.

Amanda Rodriguez is the author of DudeMom, a humor, lifestyle blog, she launched in 2008 after she had her third male child and decided to embrace life as the only princess in the house. She is now the proud mom to a teen, a tween, and a 4th grader who is wise beyond his years. In addition to chronicling her experiences as a ridiculously stylish mom of boys, Amanda owns a photography business and works full time as a digital content producer and social media manager for small businesses and startups who appreciate witty words and funny gifs as much as she does.

Alison Tedford is a busy Canadian mom who can never find her keys. She left behind cubicle life to become a freelance writer and digital marketer. She blogs on Sparklyshoesandsweatdrops.com, is on the editorial board of Bluntmoms and has been published on websites like Huffington Post, Scary Mommy, The Good Men Project, Urbanmommies and To Write Love on Her Arms. She's passionate about mental health stigma reduction, gender equality and raising quality humans. She burns cookies and enjoys long walks, but only if it's relatively flat and not rainy.

Rita Templeton is a mom trying to retain at least a shred of her pre-Mom coolness while raising her four sons (yes, four. Yes, all boys. No, she doesn't need a girl). The struggle is real, and she chronicles hers on major media outlets such as Scary Mommy, PopSugar, and HuffPost, where her words have gone viral several times over. But her favorite place to be funny is on her personal blog, Fighting Off Frumpy, which she started in 2009 at the pinnacle of her motherhood-induced frumpitude (that's a word, right?). Follow her on Facebook, Instagram, and Twitter @FightingFrumpy ... just don't send her any hate mail.

Carrie Tinsley "retired" from teaching high school English to stay home with her daughter and two sons and become the world's worst housekeeper. While her daughter attended elementary school, the boys created tents in every room, turned the back yard into a matchbox car race track, painted the stairwell "murder scene red," and once flooded the house. Carrie has struck a decent balance between being a hot mess and serving on the PTO. She loves audio books, a good beer, and writing sometimes-sweet/sometimes-sassy posts on motherhood, teaching, and current events at Carrie on Y'all (www.carrieonyall.com). You can also follow her on Facebook, Twitter, or Instagram.

Briton Underwood is a proud father of three boys. You can find his words published both online and in print under the moniker Punk Rock Papa. When not raising children or writing, he works on being a trophy husband for his beautiful wife.

Jorrie Varney is a registered nurse and mother of two who writes about the reality and insanity of parenting on her blog Close to Classy. Her parenting style can best be described as Roseanne meets Mary Poppins. Jorrie's writing has been featured on platforms such as Scary Mommy, TODAY Parents, Sammiches and Psych Meds, as well as many others. She aspires to own furniture without stains, and enjoy a shower without an audience. You can also find her on Facebook and Instagram.

Lauri Walker is wife to Brandon and mama to four kids who've managed genius status despite being raised on chicken nuggets and take out. She's the coach's wife, a sports mama, and her car smells like baseball cleats. Her words have appeared on BLUNTmoms, Mamalode, and Perfection Pending. She has regularly appeared on Today Parents Funniest Parents on Facebook and owns an amazing blog called Mama

Needs a Nap. You can find her on Facebook and Twitter. She is still trying to figure out Instagram.

Jennifer Weedon Palazzo is the creator/writer/and producer of Mom Cave TV, an online network of award-winning comedy shows. When she's not writing about the funny side of being a mom, Jennifer can be found eating Reese's Cups while bidding on vintage clothing on eBay. She splits her time between Manhattan and the Berkshires with her husband, Evan, bandleader of The Hot Sardines and their two kids. Learn more at Facebook.com/MomCaveTV, Twitter @MomCaveTV and visit https://www.youtube.com/ MomCave.

Sarah Westfall is a caffeine-dependent mom of all boys and a blogger at Life in Blue. Sarah resides in the Hoosier state with her husband Ben and their four active sons. Her blog, Life in Blue, welcomes readers into the journey (and hilarity) of trying to raise godly little dudes – one testosterone-filled story at a time. You can find out more about Sarah at Life in Blue (www.sarahwestfall.com) or follow her on Instagram (@ life_in_blue_blog) and Facebook (@lifeinblueblog).

Letter from the Editors

Thank you for reading this book. We hope you loved it. This was our first experience putting together an anthology, and we were so lucky to have an amazing squad of outstanding writers agree to join us on this journey. I hope they all know how much we appreciate each and every one of them. If you enjoyed their stories in this book make sure you check out their blogs, Facebook pages, Twitter feeds, and fabulous Instagram posts.

Raising boys is an amazing experience. There is nothing quite like the bond between a mother and a son. However, it can also be extremely difficult. Sometimes raising a boy is like living in a foreign country when you don't understand the culture or speak the language and you're pretty sure that your interpreter is drunk. For example, we still don't understand how they get pee everywhere except the toilet bowl or where all the food they eat goes. This book was created with the goal of showing what it is really like raising boys. As you can tell from our stories, every boy is unique and special in his own way and every mom is just trying her best to raise him to be a good man. It doesn't matter if you have four sons and live in a man cave or two daughters and one son you are a part of our boy mom squad and we are glad you are here.

Please tell all of your boy mom friends that they need to get this book, make this book your new go to baby shower gift for anyone pregnant with a boy, and if you are not already a member join our boy mom squad on Facebook to connect with other boy moms. If you found this book to be hilarious, heartwarming, and relatable, we would love it if you would take the time to write a review on Amazon.

XOXO

Tiffany & Lyndee

#Lifewithboys

CPSIA information can be obtained
at www.ICGtesting.com
Printed in the USA
LVHW081018030520
654907LV00002B/714